NEMOTO'S TRAVELS

The illustrated saga of a
Japanese floatplane pilot
in the first Pacific year
of the Pacific War

Michael John CLARINGBOULD

Introduction

The diary of Warrant Officer Nemoto Kumesako is a historical gem. It offers both an intimate and rare perspective of a Imperial Japanese Navy floatplane pilot early in the war, along with insights into Japanese thinking of the times. These early advances in the war were feats of considerable distance and ambition, although the incumbent technology at this distance on both sides can seem almost Steampunk.

Having spent much of my life in the Pacific I can only marvel at the distances travelled and the campaigns incurred. Today, the logistics and expenses of getting a biplane to the remote atoll of Kapingamarangi are inconceivable. The determination and skills required to navigate small floatplanes around such vast distances are considerable, and would not be contemplated today without GPS, let alone proper instrumentation. However, and surprisingly, Nemoto makes no mention of these intimidating challenges in his diary, such was the training and expectations levied upon him by his masters.

Nemoto defies every stereotype of the Japanese aviator, certainly the ones placed in front of me as a child in Papua New Guinea. Nemoto prides himself in his worldly credentials, helped by a cosmopolitan attitude then fostered within the IJN, which may surprise many. We can be sure that few other IJN pilots read Tolstoy's *War & Peace* in German for recreation. Nemoto tiptoes between the unsympathetic fates occasionally meted out to other innocents.

His fastidiousness with entering correct times and dates is a gift, and happily enable easy matching against Allied records. He never complains about his superiors or military life *per se*, and looks down on his Imperial Japanese Army counterparts, views not unique for an IJN officer. He worries about the welfare of his family and aging mother. He loses his cap on one flight and leaves his spare uniform aboard the seaplane tender *Kiyokawa Maru* when it returns to Japan for repairs. He likes the Japanese comedian Roppa and thinks, at least early on, he is fighting Vickers Wellingtons. His insights into the Tolai inhabitants around Rabaul are condescending but tainted with sympathy, and he believes they will be happier and better off under the dawning Japanese empire. He views the Japanese struggle against the British imperialists as both righteous and virtuous. Nemoto, a man of his times, has been much moulded by his military education for which he expects little in return.

Nemoto participated in many of the early Pacific War campaigns. This fact alone, combined with his unique insights, make his diary incomparable. He travelled vast distances yet regretted every time he was separated from his mother ship, the *Kiyokawa Maru*. His writing style is cultivated and matter of fact, tinged with insight and limited passion. He never envisaged it would wind up in the wrong hands, and for this reason we profit from its frankness.

I much enjoyed re-creating and illustrating Nemoto's adventures, as well as interweaving miscellaneous associated topics around the main narrative. My prying sense of humour is deliberately on display, done so to make a point, although I am first to admit some of these are obscure. Nemoto's end was as swift as it was unexpected. I hope I have done justice to him and his times, and I hope you enjoy my interpretation of his memoirs.

Michael John Claringbould
February 2021

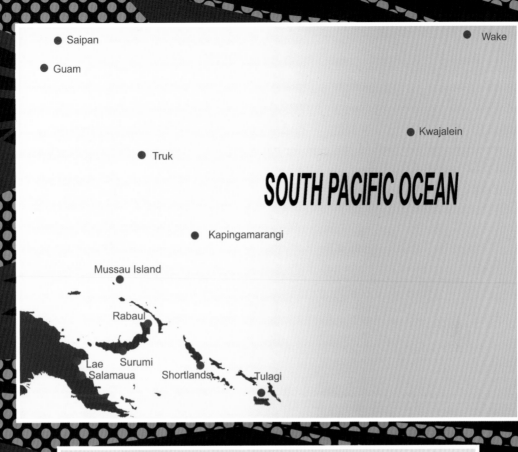

Saipan

Guam

Wake

Truk

Kwajalein

SOUTH PACIFIC OCEAN

Kapingamarangi

Mussau Island

Rabaul

Lae Surumi
Salamaua   Shortlands   Tulagi

PAPUA
and
NEW GUINEA

NEW IRELAND

Rabaul
Malaguna

NEW BRITAIN

Gasmata

Finschhafen
Lae
Salamaua

Michael Claringbould – Author & Illustrator

Michael spent his formative years in Papua New Guinea in the 1960s, during which he became fascinated by the many WWII aircraft wrecks which still lie around the country. Michael has served widely overseas as an Australian diplomat, including Southeast Asia and throughout the South Pacific where he had the fortune to return to Papua New Guinea for three years commencing in 2003. Michael has authored and illustrated various books on Pacific War aviation. His history of the Tainan Naval Air Group in New Guinea, *Eagles of the Southern Sky*, received worldwide acclaim as the first English-language history of a Japanese fighter unit, and was translated into Japanese. An executive member of Pacific Air War History Associates, Michael holds a pilot license and PG4 paraglider rating. He continues develop his skills as a digital 3D aviation artist, using in this case 3DS MAX, Vray and Photoshop to venture into the 'manga' world of comic illustration.

The author (left) with fellow paraglider pilot "Jonno", just after landing near Lake George on a 2019 winter's evening. The background paraglider is being flown by Peter Ellis.

Other Books by the Author

Black Sunday (2000)

Eagles of the Southern Sky (with Luca Ruffato, 2012)

Operation I-Go Yamamoto's Last Offensive – New Guinea and the Solomons April 1943 (Avonmore Books, 2020)

P-39 / P-400 Airacobra versus A6M2/3 Zero-sen New Guinea 1942 (Osprey, 2018)

P-47D Thunderbolt versus Ki-43 Hayabusa New Guinea 1943/44 (Osprey, 2020)

Pacific Adversaries Volume One: Japanese Army Air Force vs The Allies New Guinea 1942-1944 (Avonmore Books, 2019)

Pacific Adversaries Volume Two: Imperial Japanese Navy vs The Allies New Guinea & the Solomons 1942-1944 (Avonmore Books, 2020)

Pacific Adversaries Volume Three: Imperial Japanese Navy vs The Allies New Guinea & the Solomons 1942-1944 (Avonmore Books, 2020)

Pacific Adversaries Volume Four: Imperial Japanese Navy vs The Allies The Solomons 1942-1944 (Avonmore Books, 2021)

Pacific Profiles Volume One Japanese Army Fighters – New Guinea & the Solomons 1942-1944 (Avonmore Books, 2020)

Pacific Profiles Volume Two Japanese Army Bombers, Transports & Miscellaneous Types New Guinea & the Solomons 1942-1944 (Avonmore Books, 2020)

Pacific Profiles Volume Three Allied Medium Bombers: Douglas A-20 Havoc Series Southwest Pacific 1942-1944 (Avonmore Books, 2021)

Pacific Profiles Volume Four Allied Fighters: Vought F4U Corsair Series Solomons Theatre 1943-1944 (Avonmore Books, 2021)

Pacific Profiles Volume Five Japanese Navy Zero Fighters (land based) New Guinea and the Solomons 1942-1944 (Avonmore Books, 2021)

South Pacific Air War Volume 1: The Fall of Rabaul December 1941–March 1942 (with Peter Ingman, Avonmore Books, 2017)

South Pacific Air War Volume 2: The Struggle for Moresby March–April 1942 (with Peter Ingman, Avonmore Books, 2018)

South Pacific Air War Volume 3: Coral Sea & Aftermath May–June 1942 (with Peter Ingman, Avonmore Books, 2019)

South Pacific Air War Volume 4: Buna & Milne Bay June – September 1942 (with Peter Ingman, Avonmore Books, 2020)

OK, LISSEN PIPL. THIS EDUKATIONAL JOURNEY WILL BOTH ENTERTAIN + INFORM. YOU WILL LEARN MANY, MANY NEW THINGS.

THIS IS THE TRUE STORY OF WARRANT OFFICER NEMOTO KUMESAKO WHO SERVED ABOARD SEAPLANE TENDER KIYOKAWA MARU FROM THE BEGINNING OF THE PACIFIC WAR UNTIL THE END OF JUNE 1942.

VIA HIS CRACKING ADVENTURES, YOU WILL ALSO LEARN SPADES OF DESCRIPTIVE JAPANESE TERMS & OTHER RARE WW2 JAPANESE MILITARY TERMINOLOGY.

RARE PHOTO!

MUCH OF THE STORY CENTERS AROUND RABAUL, WITH ITS HOT SPRINGS & VOLCANOES, IT WAS OCCUPIED BY THE JAPANESE NAVY FROM 1942 TO 1945. THE KANJI OPPOSITE MEANS "KIKAN SHIKENDAI" - "ENGINE TEST STAND". THE RADIAL ENGINE IS FROM A NAKAJIMA E8N2 'DAVE' FLOATPLANE ASSIGNED TO NEMOTO'S SHIP WHILE AT RABAUL.

THE DUDE OPPOSITE WITH SAFARI HELMET IN SHARP IJN WHITES IS LT TAKEDA SHIGEKI, COMMANDER OF THE DETACHMENT. THESE GUYS ARE AT MALAGUNA NEAR RABAUL AROUND FEBRUARY 1942. YOU WILL SOON SEE MORE OF TAKEDA *ET AL.*

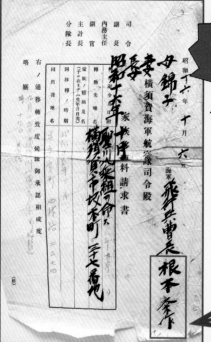

ANOTHER RARE PHOTO!

THIS VOLCANO IS CALLED TAVURUR - A WORD IN THE LOCAL TOLAI LANGUAGE FOR A HUMMING BEE. THE VOLCANO SOUNDS LIKE THIS WHEN IT RUMBLES.

THIS RIPPING YARN FAITHFULLY CITES NEMOTO'S DIARY, ALONG WITH IJN OPERATIONAL LOGS AND OTHER DOCUMENTS. NOW, CHECK OUT THE OPPOSITE EXCERPT, BEING NEMOTO'S APPLICATION TO THE COMMANDER OF YOKOSUKA NAVAL AIR GROUP TO REFUND EXPENSES FOR THE TRANSFER OF HIS WIFE KANEKO AND DAUGHTER TO YOKOSUKA WHERE HE ARRIVED 19 SEPTEMBER 1941.

HIS FAMILY FOLLOWED HIM A MONTH LATER FROM THEIR HOME AT 2374 NISHI YOKOMICHI, HIROMOTO MACHI, KURE. THIS IS HOW HE SCRIPTED HIS NAME IN KANJI.

根本粂作

WHY ?

DOES THIS BEAUTIFUL HOLLYWOOD STARLET FEATURE IN THIS CRACKING TALE?

HER NAME IS DEANNA DURBIN, A CANADIAN-BORN ACTRESS WHO WAS POPULAR IN MUSICAL FILMS THROUGHOUT THE 1930S AND 1940S. SHE HAD A DULCIT SOPRANO VOICE TOO, PERFORMING A WIDE RANGE OF STYLES FROM POPULAR SONGS TO OPERATIC ARIAS. SHE LATER SETTLED IN FRANCE, & YOU WILL SOON DISCOVER WHY SHE FEATURES IN THESE GRIPPING ADVENTURES.

SO, TO SET THE MOOD HERE IS NEMOTO DEPARTING THE LAUNCH PLATFORM ON KIYOKAWA MARU, HEADED FOR ANOTHER PATROL, SOME OF WHICH PROVED MUCH MORE ADVENTUROUS THAN OTHERS.

AT THIS JUNCTURE BOTH EXPLANATION & ELABORATION ARE IN ORDER, SO YOU CAN APPREICATE HOW NEMOTO WOUND UP IN THE VAST PACIFIC, SO FAR AWAY FROM HIS HOME IN KURE, JAPAN

NEMOTO'S NAKAJIMA E8N2 'DAVE' FLOATPLANE

SECRET

DIMENSIONS
LENGTH 8.81 METRES
WINGSPAN 11 METRES
MAX WEIGHT 1,900 KG

PERFORMANCE
CRUISE 100 KNOTS
MAX SPEED 160 KNOTS
RANGE 486 NAUTICAL MILES

ARMAMENT
2 X 7.7 MM MACHINE GUNS
2 X 30KG BOMBS

AFTER GRADUATING AS A PILOT, NEMOTO FIRST SERVED WITH THE YOKOSUKA
NAVAL AIR GROUP. THIS IS ONE OF THEIR EARLY DAVES IN ITS PRE-WAR LIVERY.
THE LETTER 'ヨ', WHICH LOOKS LIKE A BACKWARDS 'E', IS THE KATAKANA LETTER
PRONOUNCED 'YO', REPRESENTING YOKOSUKA

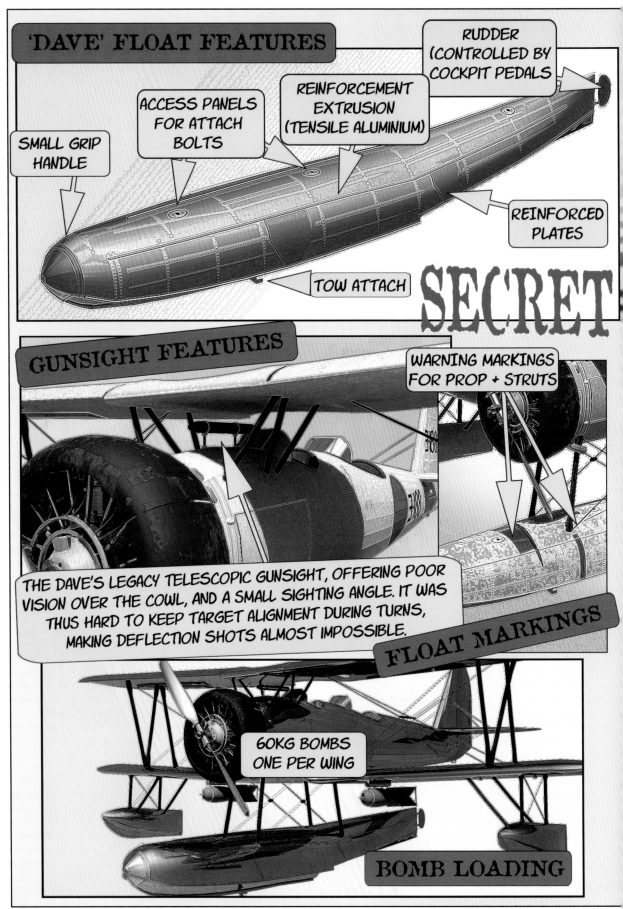

'DAVE' FLOAT FEATURES

RUDDER (CONTROLLED BY COCKPIT PEDALS

REINFORCEMENT EXTRUSION (TENSILE ALUMINIUM)

ACCESS PANELS FOR ATTACH BOLTS

SMALL GRIP HANDLE

REINFORCED PLATES

TOW ATTACH

SECRET

GUNSIGHT FEATURES

WARNING MARKINGS FOR PROP + STRUTS

THE DAVE'S LEGACY TELESCOPIC GUNSIGHT, OFFERING POOR VISION OVER THE COWL, AND A SMALL SIGHTING ANGLE. IT WAS THUS HARD TO KEEP TARGET ALIGNMENT DURING TURNS, MAKING DEFLECTION SHOTS ALMOST IMPOSSIBLE.

FLOAT MARKINGS

60KG BOMBS ONE PER WING

BOMB LOADING

THIS PAGE HAS LOTS OF DETAIL, SO STICK WITH IT.

NOTE 'K' ON FUNNEL TO REPRESENT 'KAWASAKI'

KIYOKAWA MARU IN THE PANAMA CANAL PRE-WAR

KIYOKAWA MARU WAS A 17-KNOT, 6,800-TON SHIP COMPLETED IN 1937 FOR THE KAWASAKI KISEN LINE, THEN CONVERTED TO AN AUXILIARY SEAPLANE TENDER. DUE TO ITS LACK OF ARMOUR, SLOW SPEED & MINIMAL DEFENSIVE ORDNANCE SHIPS IN ITS CLASS WERE ASSIGNED TO SUPPORT OPERATIONS AS REQUIRED. THEIR FLOATPLANES WERE LIMITED BY OPERATIONAL CONSTRAINTS; LAUNCHING FROM SEA CATAPAULTS WAS RISKY, AND OCEAN SWELLS MADE LAUNCH & RETRIEVAL CHALLENGING. FLOATPLANES MOSTLY OFFERED CLOSE AIR SUPPORT & RECONNAISSANCE DURING LANDING OPERATIONS, AND LONG-RANGE PATROLS.

AFTER LOADING ITS FLOATPLANES AT YOKOSUKA IN OCTOBER 1941, THE SHIP SAILED FOR SAIPAN ON 2 DECEMBER. BUNTAICHO LT TAKEDA SHIGEKI COMMANDED 4 X NAKAJIMA E8N2 DAVES, 2 X MITSUBISHI F1M2 PETES & 3 X AICHI E13A1 JAKE FLOATPLANES. AS MOST SENIOR OFFICER, TAKEDA ASSIGNED HIMSELF A PETE, THE FASTEST AND MOST MODERN TYPE ABOARD. OPPOSITE IS ONE OF THE DAVE PILOTS OVER RABAUL IN FEBRUARY 1942. ITS NOT NEMOTO, SO MUST BE ONE OF THE OTHER THREE DAVE PILOTS AT THE TIME; FPO2c AOSHIMA SHOZABURO, FPO2c SHIBATA SHOJI OR FPO3c KASAI SHIGEO.

THE IJN WAS RAISED AND TRAINED BY HER MAJESTY'S BRITISH NAVY. EARLY OPERATIONS UNDERWAY . . .

THIS IS HOW A DAVE IS HOISTED ABOARD

13

BACK IN THE EARLY 1990s THE ANIMATION 'PORCO ROSSO' CAPTIVATED MANY. YOU MUST SEE THIS FILM. IT WAS CREATED BY JAPANESE ANIMATOR, SCREENWRITER & AUTHOR MIYAZAKI HAYAO WHOSE FILM CLEARLY DEFINES HISTORICAL AND GEOGRAPHICAL SETTINGS, SET ALONG THE PICTURESQUE ADRIATIC COAST. THE MAIN CHARACTER PORCO CLEVERLY MAKES ANTI-FASCIST STATEMENTS THROUGHOUT.

ALTHOUGH OUR HERO NEMOTO IS APOLITICAL, HE DEFIES THE JAPANESE MILITARIST STEREOTYPE. YOU WILL COME TO BE ENLIGHTENED INTO HIS PHILOSOPHY INCLUDING WHY HE TASKS SUBORDINATES TO POLISH HIS SWORD!

ON 25 NOVEMBER 1941 NEMOTO WATCHED FLOATPLANES BEING LOADED ABOARD KIYOKAKWA MARU WHEN DOCKED AT YOKOSUKA. THIS IS HOW THE SHIP APPEARED BEFORE IT HAD MILITARY GREY APPLIED. LOOK CAREFULLY AND YOU CAN SEE SEVERAL FLOATPLANES ALREADY LOADED ABOARD.

ON 28 NOVEMBER THE SHIP SAILED BUT SOON HIT ROUGH SEAS. WHEN THE MAIN ENGINE BRIEFLY FAILED BELOW DECK A STORED DAVE FLOATPLANE WAS DAMAGED. THE SHIP FINALLY ANCHORED OFF SAIPAN LATE 2 DECEMBER.

AT 0720 HOURS ON 7 DECEMBER THE SHIP'S COMPANY WAS READ AN IMPERIAL EDICT ISSUED BY COMMANDER OF THE COMBINED FLEET. IT PROCLAIMED THAT JAPAN WOULD **DECLARE WAR** AGAINST THE UNITED STATES AT 0800 NEXT MORNING.

NEMOTO'S FIRST MISSION ON DAY ONE OF THE WAR

"A GREAT SUCCESS"

THE EDICT CONCLUDED: *"FLEET RESPONSIBILITIES WILL BE VERY HEAVY & THE OUTCOME WILL DICTATE OUR COUNTRY'S FATE. YOU HAVE MASTERED ACHIEVEMENTS TRHOUGH FLEET DISCIPLINE FOR A LONG TIME, BUT NOW DETERMINATION IS REQUIRED TO EXALT IMPERIAL AUTHORITY THROUGHOUT THE WORLD BY ANNIHILATING THE ENEMY".* **THE SHIP'S FLOATPLANES LAUNCHED FROM SAIPAN AT 0630, IN THREE FLIGHTS LED BY LT TAKEDA SHIGEKI. THE SECOND FLIGHT OF FOUR DAVES WAS LED BY NEMOTO ACCOMPANIED BY FPO2c AOSHIMA SHOZABURO, FPO2c SHIBATA SHOJI AND FPO3c KASAI SHIGEO. THE THIRD FLIGHT WAS THREE JAKES**

THE 'STANDARD OIL' TANK FARM DESTROYED

ON 8 DECEMBER THE NINE FLOATPLANES ATTACKED GUAM AT 0827 DESTROYING FUEL TANKS AND MARINE BARRACKS. THEY ALSO BOMBED THE PAN AIR HOTEL AND PITI NAVY YARD, CAUSING MUCH DAMAGE.

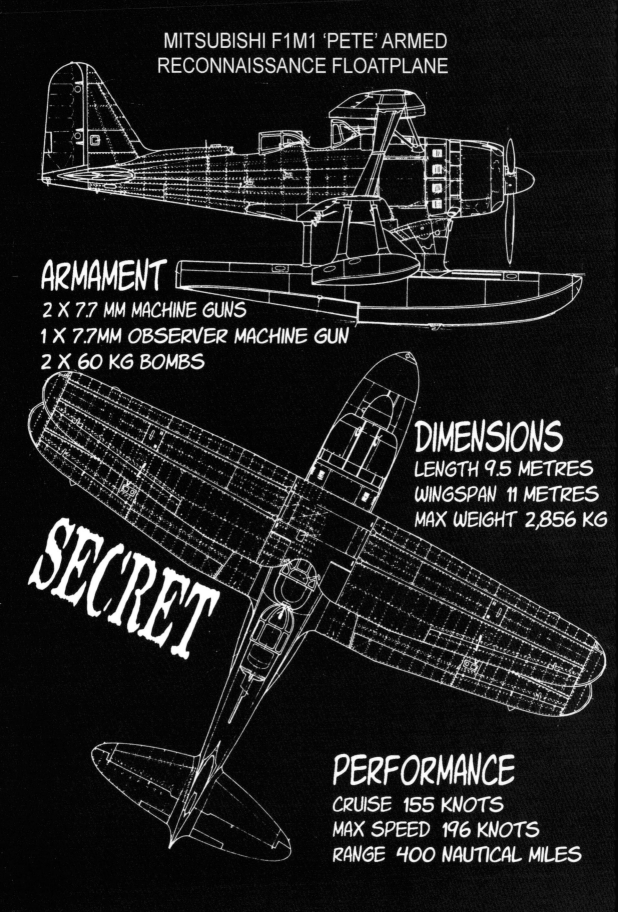

MITSUBISHI F1M1 'PETE' ARMED RECONNAISSANCE FLOATPLANE

ARMAMENT
2 X 7.7 MM MACHINE GUNS
1 X 7.7MM OBSERVER MACHINE GUN
2 X 60 KG BOMBS

DIMENSIONS
LENGTH 9.5 METRES
WINGSPAN 11 METRES
MAX WEIGHT 2,856 KG

SECRET

PERFORMANCE
CRUISE 155 KNOTS
MAX SPEED 196 KNOTS
RANGE 400 NAUTICAL MILES

LT TAKEDA SHIGEKI LEADS THE FIRST MISSION OF THE WAR

AT END OFTHE ATTACK THE NINE PURSUED MINESWEEPER USS PENGUIN, JUST RETURNED FROM A PATROL. SEVERAL BOMBS STRADDLED THE SHIP, KILLING ONE SAILOR & WOUNDING SEVERAL.

NEMOTO WORE HIS 'THOUSAND STICHES' BELLY SASH, A GIFT FROM HIS WIFE, VIEWING THE MISSION "A GREAT SUCCESS". TAKEDA THEN LED THE FLOATPLANES BACK TO THE SHIP. THE FOLLOWING DAY AT 1730 HOURS THE ENTIRE SHIP'S CREW ASSEMBLED WHERE COMMANDER TAKAHASHI NOBUYOSHI TOLD THEM THAT JAPAN HAD DECLARED WAR THE DAY PREVIOUS.

THE THREE JAKES WERE LED BY WO KOSAKI YOSHIYUKI

"A USEFUL PHRASE"

Variable Pitch Propeller
可變螺步螺旋機
kahen raho rasenki

KOSAKI'S GUNNER STOWS HIS MACHINE-GUN ON RETURN

TAKAHASHI WAS HIKOTAICHO OF NO 18 NAVAL AIR GROUP, ALSO OPERATING JAKES. HIS UNIT WAS SIMILARLY INVOLVED IN THE SAME OPERATIONS AS THE HEROIC FLYERS FROM KIYOKAWA MARU.

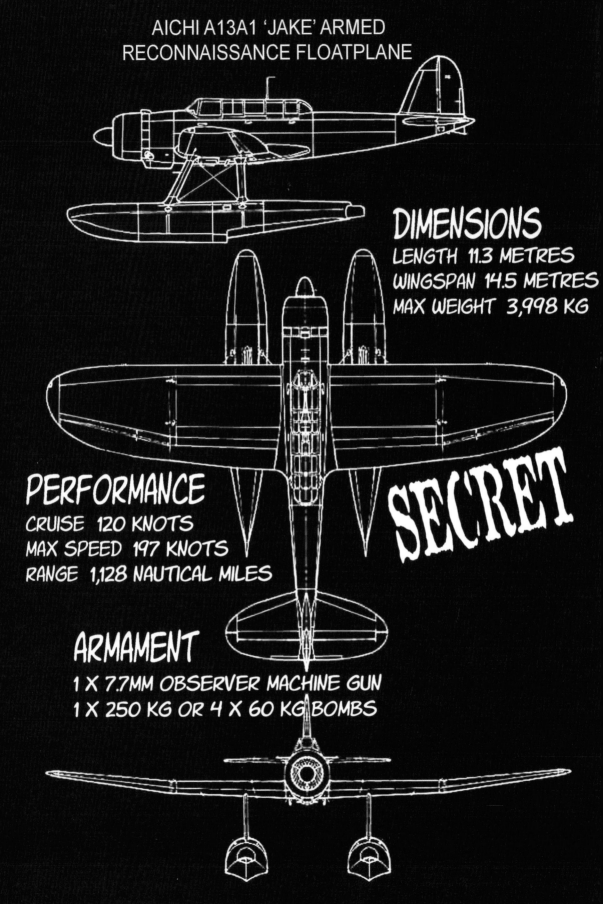

AICHI A13A1 'JAKE' ARMED RECONNAISSANCE FLOATPLANE

DIMENSIONS
LENGTH 11.3 METRES
WINGSPAN 14.5 METRES
MAX WEIGHT 3,998 KG

PERFORMANCE
CRUISE 120 KNOTS
MAX SPEED 197 KNOTS
RANGE 1,128 NAUTICAL MILES

SECRET

ARMAMENT
1 X 7.7MM OBSERVER MACHINE GUN
1 X 250 KG OR 4 X 60 KG BOMBS

NEMOTO LAUNCHES AT 0330 ON HIS LAST GUAM MISSION

ON 10 DECEMBER NEMOTO LED HIS DAVE FLIGHT DURING THE IJN OCCUPATION OF GUAM. THEY LEFT PORT OMIYA AT 0330 HOURS, HOWEVER UPON ARRIVAL AN HOUR LATER THE LANDING WAS OVER. THE OPERATION TOOK LESS TIME THAN EXPECTED & ALL AIRCREW WERE GIVEN TWO DAYS REST.

SUCCESS!

KIYOKAWA MARU

WITH THE GUAM CAMPAIGN SUCCESSFULLY CONCLUDED, NEMOTO AND HIS PALS PACKED UP THEIR FLOATPLANES ON 12 DECEMBER. IT TOOK THEM JUST OVER SEVEN HOURS TO LOAD, STOW AND SECURE ALL NINE.

"ANOTHER USEFUL PHRASE"

「アネロイド」高度計

THE KATAKANA [IN BRACKETS] READS "ANEROIDO", + THE KANJI "KODOKEI" ("ALTIMETER") GIVING "ANEROID ALTIMETER", AN INDISPENSIBLE TERM WHEN RESTORING YOUR A6M ZERO

NEMOTO & HIS LOYAL COMRADES ARE HEADED FOR TRUK

TRUK WAS BEING GOVERNED BY THE EMPIRE OF JAPAN UNDER A MANDATE FROM THE LEAGUE OF NATIONS. THIS FOLLOWED GERMANY'S DEFEAT IN WORLD WAR I, AS A PRIZE FOR FIGHTING WITH THE ALLIES. TRUK ATOLL BOASTS A PROTECTIVE REEF OF 225 KILOMETRES CIRCUMFERENCE WHICH PORTENDS A VAST NATURAL HARBOUR OF A MASSIVE 2,120 SQUARE KILOMETRES !

YESSIR !

WAKE ME UP WHEN WE GET THERE AIRMAN

SEVERAL IJN RECONNAISSANCE FLIGHTS WERE MADE IN DECEMBER 1941 AGAINST RABAUL AND KAVIENG BY THE LUMBERING GIANTS OF THE YOKOHAMA NAVAL AIR GROUP. THESE FOUR-ENGINED H6K4 'MAVIS' FLYING BOATS WERE STILL IN PRE-WAR ALUMINIUM LIVERY.

THESE WERE LONG FLIGHTS OF ABOUT TEN HOURS DURATION.

... OF BOREDOM

HOURS + HOURS + MORE HOURS

THE MIGHTY H6K4 MAVIS FOUR-ENGINED FLYING BOAT

ON 13 DECEMBER KIYOKAWA MARU SAILED FOR TRUK AT 0800 HOURS. ALTHOUGH MOST FLOATPLANES WERE SECURED ON DECK, ONE DAVE WAS STORED BELOW WITH FOLDED WINGS. BOTH WINGS FOLDED BACK AT 90 DEGREES AFTER THE FORWARD SPAR BOLTS WERE DETACHED.

SECURED BELOW DECK IN THIS FASHION, AWAY FROM THE ELEMENTS, THE FLOATPLANES COULD RECEIVE PROPER MAINTENANCE FROM THE MANY SPARES ALSO KEPT ABOARD.

FOLDING STORAGE BELOW DECKS FOR DAVES

THE SHIP ARRIVED AT TRUK MID-AFTERNOON OF 15 DECEMBER WHERE THE CREW IS TOLD THEY WILL DEPART FOR KWAJALEIN THE NEXT DAY. THE VOYAGE IS RELATIVELY SMOOTH AND THOSE FLOATPLANES SECURED ON DECK REMAIN UNDAMAGED. THE DAVE IS THE SLOWEST IN THE SHIP'S INVENTORY, ABOUT WHICH WE SHALL SOON HEAR NEMOTO'S OPINION. HE & HIS PALS ARE MAKING QUICK PROGRESS THROUGH THE PACIFIC. ON THESE LONG VOYAGES HE HAS TIME TO REMINISCE, REVEALING THE INNER PHILOSOPHER . . .

QUOTING NEMOTO'S DIARY

16 December 1941

However our ship, brandishing the sword of justice, advances to the east and to the west with no time to spare. Silently, we advance. How far? There is no love, no romance where a man goes. Conquering the seas we arrive at enemy islands . . . the battle ends in an instant, everything like a dream. When sitting at the base writing a diary I realise, for the first time, that I am still alive and embrace my existance. Trhis is the road along which men march.

ON 21 DECEMBER THE SHIP SAILED FOR WAKE. UPON ARRIVAL ITS JAKES & PETES LAUNCHED AT 0430. NEMOTO'S THREE DAVES WERE ON STANDBY AND DID NOT PARTICPATE IN THE BRIEF COMBAT. THE SHIP WAS MEANT TO RETRIEVE THE OTHER FLOATPLANES FROM POKWAKU ISLAND, HOWEVER A HUGE SWELL PREVENTED THIS, AND INSTEAD THEY COLLECTED THEM FROM KWAJALEIN. ON 25 DECEMBER NEMOTO PATROLLED AROUND EBEJE ISLAND WHERE THAT EVENING WITH OTHER PILOTS HE COMMEMORATED EMPORER TAISHO. ON 29 DECEMBER HE RETURNED TO NO. 17 NAVAL AIR GROUP HQ AT TRUK, FLEW AN ANTI-SUBMARINE PATROL, THEN RETURNED TO TRUK. THE NEXT DAY KIYOKAWA MARU ALSO RETURNED TO TRUK JUST AFTER LUNCH. NEMOTO SPENT THE LAST DAY OF THE YEAR HERE.

EMPEROR TAISHO WAS THE 123rd EMPEROR OF JAPAN & PASSED AWAY ON 25 DECEMBER 1926. ON THE LEFT ARE HIS FOUR SONS IN 1921; HIROHITO, TAKAHITO, NOBUHITO & YASUHITO. HIROHITO SUCCEEDED HIS FATHER TO BECOME THE NEXT AND WARTIME EMPEROR. TAISHO IS DEPICTED IN THIS MEIJI ERA LITHOGRAPH ON THE RIGHT (CIRCLED)

31 DEC 41

"This past year has brought so many changes, and I thank the Gods for delivering me safely. I am resolved to do my utmost until such time as our national prestige will be crowned by glory."

NEMOTO'S LAST DIARY ENTRY FOR 1941

NEMOTO BETRAYS HIS SOFT SIDE WHEN HE CONTINUES, *"THE HEARTS OF THE DEFENDERS OF WAKE & THEIR FAMILIES MUST BE FULL OF DEEP EMOTION. I FEEL SYMPATHETIC DESPITE THE FACT THEY ARE OUR ENEMY . . . PITY YOUR ENEMY BUT HATE HIS DEEDS"*

THE FIRST DAY OF 1942 FOUND NEMOTO AND HIS PALS AT TRUK UNDERGOING AIR COMBAT TRAINING ON A5M4 CLAUDE FIGHTERS WITH THE CHITOSE NAVAL AIR GROUP AT TAKEJIMA AIR BASE ON ETEN ISLAND. HERE THEY SHARED BARRACKS WITH OTHER FLOATPLANE PILOTS FROM NO. 17 NAVAL AIR GROUP WHO TRAINED SIMILARLY. THE TRAINING WENT ON ALL HOURS, AND NEMOTO WAS OF THE OPINION THAT IT DID *"A LOT OF GOOD"*.

THEN, JUST WHEN EVERYTHING WAS PEACHY, THE RAAF & THEIR PESKY HUDSONS BOMBED A SMALL ATOLL A LOOONG WAY AWAY CALLED GREENWICH ISLAND. THE EXCITING NEWS ELECTRIFIED TRUK NAVAL COMMAND! SO, ON 8 JANUARY NEMOTO SUDDENLY FOUND HIMSELF ON A MAVIS FLYING BOAT BOUND FOR THE REMOTE ATOLL. JUST BEFORE HE BOARDED HE WROTE, "AT LAST I AM FLYING TO GREENWICH BY FLYING BOAT AT 1300 TODAY! *WHAT FATE IS AWAITING US THERE! WE ONLY HAVE TO THINK OF OUR COUNTRY*". KNOW THAT GREENWICH ISLAND WAS ALSO KNOWN AS KAPINGAMARANGI.

ESPIONAGE!

YOU MUST FIRST KNOW THE ATOLL'S HISTORY. FOR MANY YEARS THE JAPANESE MILITARY HAD BEEN AWARE OF THE STRATEGIC VALUE OF KAPINGAMARANGI, AND ON 3 JULY 1937 THE SPECIAL SERVICE VESSEL KOSHU HAD TRANSPORTED METEOROLOGISTS THERE IN ORDER TO CONDUCT GEOGRAPHIC, MAPPING & METEOROLOGICAL SURVEYS. UNDER INTERNATIONAL LAW THE ATOLL WAS THEN PART OF THE JAPANESE EMPIRE, SO THE JAPANESE BROKE NO RULES CONDUCTING SUCH ACTIVITY.

NOT SO THE AUSTRALIANS HOWEVER . . . READ ON !

MORE ESPIONAGE !

DEUCED DIFFICULT TO SEE UNDER THAT THICK OVERCAST SIR

Radio silence . . .

ON 17 JUNE 1941, SEVERAL MONTHS BEFORE THE DECLARATION OF WAR, THREE RAAF HUDSONS (A16-13/ 16 & 91) DEPARTED TOWNSVILLE FOR A SECRET MISSION. THEY PROCEEDED TO RABAUL THEN KAVIENG WHERE THEY CONDUCTED (QUOTING SQUADRON RECORDS), *"SEARCHES AND PHOTOGRAPHIC RECONNAISSANCES".*

IN FACT, THE HUDSONS CONDUCTED ILLEGAL FLIGHTS OVER KAPINGAMARANGI. LOW CLOUD PRECLUDED DETAILED OBSERVATION. IT IS UNCLEAR WHICH LEVEL OF GOVERNMENT AUTHORISED THE FLIGHT. THE ROYAL AUSTRALIAN NAVY INTELLIGENCE OFFICE IN PORT MORESBY SUBSEQUENTLY COMPLAINED TO RAAF HEADQUARTERS, MELBOURNE, THAT THE MISSION *"OBTAINED NO USEFUL INTELLIGENCE AND IN RETURN VIOLATED JAPANESE NEUTRALITY, AND LOST THE FUTURE ELEMENT OF SURPRISE".* OUCH !

ON 2 DECEMBER 1941, GOSHU MARU DELIVERED SEVERAL FLOATPLANES AND MATERIEL TO THE ATOLL. THEN, THROUGHOUT JANUARY 1942 MINELAYER KOEI MARU (OPPOSITE) OPERATED SUPPLY SHUTTLES BETWEEN TRUK & KAPINGAMARANGI, THE FIRST VOYAGE ARRIVING THERE ON 2 JANUARY 1942.

THE FIRST THING THE JAPANESE BUILT WAS AN OBSERVATION TOWER TO LOOKOUT FOR ENEMY AIRCRAFT. THE GOSHU MARU RETURNED AGAIN IN MID-DECEMBER BRINGING MORE BUILDING MATERIALS FROM WHICH THEY BUILT TWO CEMENT SLIPWAYS FOR FLOATPLANES TO ACCESS SHORE MAINTENANCE. OTHER SUPPLIES INCLUDED FUEL TANKS SO THAT LONG-RANGE MAVIS FLYING BOATS COULD USE THE ATOLL TO REFUEL. BARGES FROM TRUK BROUGHT MORE MATERIALS TOO. THE IJN WAS DETERMINED TO CONVERT THE ATOLL INTO A VIABLE OUTPOST.

HUDSON A16-47

THEN ON 15 DECEMBER 1941, FROM RABAUL RAAF NO. 24 SQUADRON HUDSON A16-39 RECONNOITRED THE ATOLL FLOWN BY FLT-LT KEN ERWIN (THE ATOLL WAS NO STRANGER TO ERWIN WHO HAD PREVIOUSLY FLOWN THE SPY FLIGHT TO KAPINGAMARANGI BACK IN JUNE 1941). ERWIN MADE TWO PHOTO RUNS BEFORE BOMBING GOSHU MARU.
THE MERCHANTMAN RETURNED FIRE THEN BROKE MOORINGS TO ESCAPE.

NEAR MISS !

ERWIN REPORTED NINE BARGES & OTHER VESSELS AS WELL AS THE TWO NEW CEMENT SLIPWAYS. BACK AT RABAUL HE ASSEMBLED THREE MORE CREWS FOR A RETURN ATTACK LED FROM HUDSON A16-47, ALONG WITH A16-13 & A16-91 FLOWN BY FLT-LTS J MURPHY AND P. PATERSON, BOTH ALSO VETERANS OF THE JUNE 1941 SPY FLIGHT. THEY FOUND GOSHU MARU IN FULL RETREAT 20 MILES NORTH OF KAPINGAMARANGI. ALL THEIR BOMBS MISSED THE FLEEING SHIP AT 1637 HOURS, AND THEY FLEW HOME IN PITCH DARKNESS, LANDING AT RABAUL AT 2100.

LOCKHEED HUDSON MKI

DIMENSIONS
LENGTH 13.5 METRES
WINGSPAN 20 METRES
MAX WEIGHT 7,935 KG

SECRET

ARMAMENT
2 X .303 MACHINE GUNS (NOSE)
2 X .303 MACHINE GUNS (TURRET)

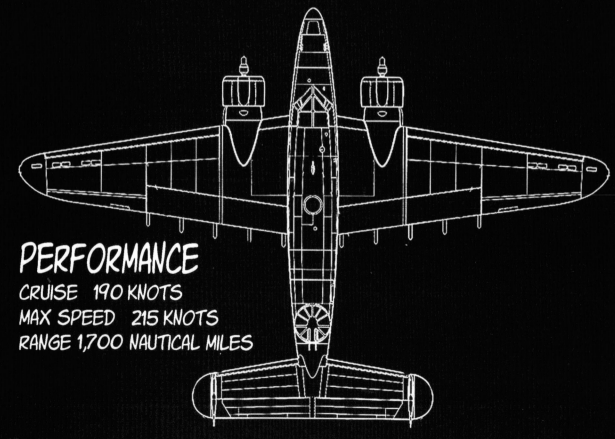

PERFORMANCE
CRUISE 190 KNOTS
MAX SPEED 215 KNOTS
RANGE 1,700 NAUTICAL MILES

SPECIAL LIEUTENANT
NAKASHIMA CHU'UROKU
(中島忠六)

BACK AT TRUK, HIKOCHO OF 17 NAVAL AIR GROUP, COMMANDER YAMAMOTO SAKAE, AUTHORISED REINFORCEMENT FLOATPLANES TO GREENWICH ATOLL ON 16 DECEMBER 1941. THE ATOLL IS NAMED グリニシケ IN KATAKANA ('GURINISHIKE' TO REPLICATE THE NAME 'GREENWICH'). MANY YEARS AGO SOME HISTORIAN WRONGLY TRANSLATED THIS AS 'GURINISHIMA' MEANING GREEN ISLAND. TO THIS DAY YOU WILL FIND RECORDS WRONGLY CLAIMING THIS WAS THE NAME ACCORDED TO THE ATOLL BY THE JAPANESE. THIS IS DEEPLY REGRETTABLE & INCORRECT.

ON 16 DECEMBER SPECIAL LIEUTENANT NAKASHIMA CHU'UROKU DEPARTED TRUK JUST BEFORE LUNCH LEADING TWO FLIGHTS OF THREE JAKE FLOATPLANES BOUND FOR グリニシケ. WITH NO NAVIGATION AIDS, FINDING THE DISTANT SPECK IN THE VAST PACIFIC WAS ALWAYS CHALLENGING, AND ON THIS OCCASION NAKASHMA'S SIX MACHINES RELUCTANTLY RETURNED HOME AT 1400 UPON ENCOUNTERING BAD WEATHER.

中島の航空機 (Nakashima's aircraft)

グリニシケ

NAKASHIMA'S SIX JAKES GOT TO THE ATOLL SUCCESSFULLY NEXT MORNING OF WEDNESDAY 17 DECEMBER, LAUNCHING FROM TRUK HARBOUR AT 0700 WITH THE SAME CREWS. WITH A MINOR DETOUR FOR WEATHER, THEY SAFELY ALIGHTED AT 'GURINISHIKE' AT 1030.

EARLY NEXT MORNING . . .

THE NEW CONTINGENT'S FIRST PATROL LASTED NEARLY SIX HOURS, DEPARTING FIRST THING NEXT MORNING OF 18 DEC AT 0517 HOURS, LED BY NAKASHIMA & ACCOMPANIED BY WO ISHIKAWA YOSHIO. THEY LANDED JUST BEFORE 1100 AND TOOK AN HOUR FOR LUNCH. THE PAIR DEPARTED AGAIN AT 1230 FOR ANOTHER PATROL, THIS TIME MUCH MORE EVENTFUL . . .

SQN LDR JOHN LEREW LED THE NEXT MISSION TO KAPINGAMARANGI ON 18 DECEMBER. AS HE GUIDED HUDSON A16-91 OVER THE ATOLL, HE WAS ATTACKED BY NAKASHIMA'S TWO JAKES ON THEIR SECOND PATROL OF THE DAY AT 1230. NAKASHIMA'S REAR GUNNER FIRED AT LEREW WHO RETURNED FIRE WITH HIS TWIN 30 CALIBRE NOSE GUNS.

LEREW REPORTED THAT THE JAKE QUICKLY BROKE OFF CONTACT, & DOWN BELOW HE SAW AN ESTIMATED ONE THOUSAND PEOPLE ON THE BIGGEST ISLAND: THIS NUMBER WAS OVERLY-AMBITIOUS, HOWEVER THERE WERE IN FACT LOTS OF CURIOUS & HAPPY ISLANDERS ENJOYING THE AERIAL SPECTACLE, POINTING AT THE SKY, AND SHOUTING WITH GLEE.

✱FACT: NEARLY ALL IJN PILOTS THOUGH THEY WERE FIGHTING BRITISH FORCES. THEY HAD NO IDEA WHO AUSTRALIANS WERE.

ON 20 DECEMBER THE GALLANT ERWIN RETURNED, REPORTING SMUGLY THAT HE ESCAPED YET ANOTHER FLOATPLANE ATTACK DUE TO SUPERIOR SPEED. THE BELIGERANT WAS ONE OF FOUR JAKES. THEN, ON CHRISTMAS DAY THE RAAF MADE ITS FINAL ATTACK FOR 1941 WHEN TWO HUDSONS DIVE-BOMBED THE ATOLL, THIS TIME RESISTED BY ONE JAKE & ONE PETE WHICH FIRED AT THEM AT 1020 HOURS, BUT WITH NO RESULTS. REGRETTABLY THE FLOATPLANE CREWS ARE NOT RECORDED IN THE RELEVANT OPERATIONS LOG.

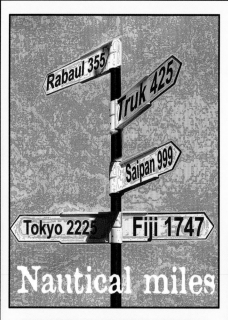

Rabaul 355
Truk 425
Saipan 999
Tokyo 2225
Fiji 1747

Nautical miles

Here is the IJN phrase for "aeronautical meteorology"

航空気象学
(Kokukishogaku)

KAPINGAMARANGI WAS TRULY IN THE MIDDLE OF NOWHERE. CHECK OUT THE SIGNPOST OPPOSITE !

TOWARD YEAR'S END ON 29 DECEMBER 1941, KIYOKAWA MARU SAILED FROM TRUK MID-MORNING BOUND FOR THIS DISTANT ATOLL WHERE IT UNLOADED SEVERAL FLOATPLANES, ONE BEING AN OBSOLETE E7K RECONNAISSANCE 'ALF' - SEE ITS KANJI DESIGNATION BELOW. THE TYPE HAD BEGAN SERVICE IN 1935, BUT ITS PERFORMANCE WAS HINDERED BY THE UNRELIABILITY OF ITS HIRO ENGINE.

九四式水上偵察機
Type 94 Reconnaissance Floatplane

Kapingamarangi Tales
How to Repair Seaplanes on an Atoll
The Great Kapingamarangian
The Ethics of Engaging Hudsons
A Tale of Two Floatplanes
Kapingamarangi Revisited
The Catcher in the Sky
One flew over the Atoll
Lord of the Lakes
Brave New Whirl

WITH SUCH EXCITEMENT CURRENTLY FOCUSSED AROUND KAPINGAMARANGI, CONTEMPLATE THE THE OPPOSITE BOOK TITLES AND THEIR LITERARY PROMISE.

"ANOTHER USEFUL PHRASE"

An important term to learn for IJN floatplane operations is 'aircraft catapult'

航空機發出機
(kokuki hashutsuki)

FOR SUCH A REMOTE ATOLL, THIS PICTURESQUE PIECE OF GEOGRAPHY WAS ABOUT TO RECEIVE LOTS OF ATTENTION. ON THE FIRST DAY OF 1942, SQUADRON LEADER LEREW RETURNED WITH FOUR HUDSONS & BOMBED THE FLEDGLING JAPANESE BASE.

HE REPORTED THAT A TALL COLUMN OF THICK, BLACK SMOKE INDICATED A FUEL DUMP HAD BEEN HIT. ALL HUDSONS RETURNED SAFELY TO RABAUL AFTER A ROUND TRIP OF FIVE & A HALF HOURS.

WHERE THE HELL ARE THEY? DANG, THIS IS SOOOOO DAAAAARK!

THE ENGLISH IMPERIALIST INTRUDERS WILL NOT ESCAPE NEXT TIME!

THE ONLY 'ALF' ON THE ATOLL . . .

TWO DAYS LATER LEREW LED THREE HUDSONS BACK TO THE ATOLL DEPARTING RABAUL IN THE DARK AT 0135 IN ORDER TO ARRIVE OVER TARGET BEFORE DAWN. THEY MADE LOW-LEVEL PASSES OVER THE NEW CEMENT SLIPWAYS. AT 0340 HOURS THE ONLY RESISTANCE WAS THE SOLE ALF LAUNCHED IN A FUTILE GESTURE OF DEFIANCE. THE HUDSON CREWS DID NOT EVEN SEE IT. THE ANTIQUATED BIPLANE FAILED TO CATCH THE RAIDERS, & TWO GROUND CREW WERE KILLED IN THE ATTACK.

"ANOTHER USEFUL EXPLIQUÉ"

Did you know? Many IJN aeronautical terms were borrowed from English and transliterated in Katakana, like the term for 'float' rendered as 'furoto' フロート

ON 6 JANUARY LEREW AGAIN PROVED A MAJOR NUISANCE WHEN HE LED TWO HUDSONS BACK TO THE ATOLL. RAAF BOMBS DESTROYED A JAKE ON THE SLIPWAY. THE OPERATIONAL LOG FOR 17 NAVAL AIR GROUP NOTES THAT THE BOMBERS *"APPROACHED VERY CLOSE TO THE OBSERVATION TOWER & FIRED AT IT."*

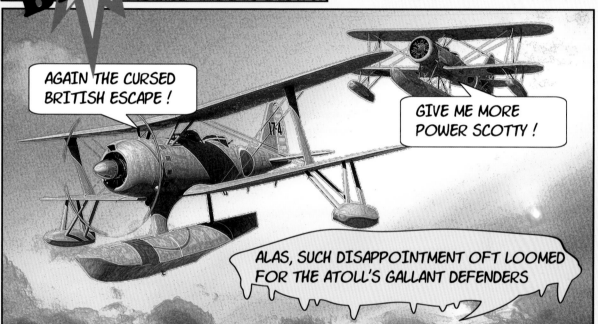

AGAIN THE CURSED BRITISH ESCAPE !

GIVE ME MORE POWER SCOTTY !

ALAS, SUCH DISAPPOINTMENT OFT LOOMED FOR THE ATOLL'S GALLANT DEFENDERS

THIS TIME A PETE & DAVE SCRAMBLED IMMEDIATELY FROM THEIR MOORINGS AND CHASED THE TWO FLEEING BOMBERS. THE OPERATIONS LOG UNFORTUNATELY ONLY RECORDS SURNAMES;

PETE PILOT FPO1c NOZAWA 能澤 WITH OBSERVER FLYER1c SATO 佐藤, AND

DAVE PILOT FPO2c SHIBATA FPO2c 柴田 WITH OBSERVER FPO2c MITSUSHIRO 三代

BUT HELP IS ON THE WAY, IN THE FORM OF TWO MAVIS FROM YOKOHAMA NAVAL AIR GROUP COMMANDED BY LT NAGASHIMA SABURO. THE PAIR IS BRINGING MORE BRAVE FLOATPLANE PILOTS INCLUDING OUR HERO, WO NEMOTO KUMESAKO!

ARE WE THERE YET?

WAKE UP COMRADES! WE ARE ALMOST THERE!

NEMOTO ARRIVED AT THE PICTURESQUE ATOLL ON AFTERNOON OF 8 JANUARY AFTER A FOUR-HOUR FLIGHT FROM TRUK WHICH HAD DEPARTED JUST AFTER LUNCH. HE LAMENTED *"I DID NOT BRING MY LUNCH AND HAD TO FEED ON CAKES AND CIDER OFFERED TO ME BY SUBORDINATES".* NEMOTO SOON DISCOVERED THAT THE MEN ON THE ATOLL HAD LIMITED FRESH WATER AND WERE RELUCTANT TO SHAVE, NONETHELESS HAPPILY MORALE WAS HIGH !

WOW BEAUTIFUL SCENERY! CAN WE STAY LONGER HERE LT NAGASHIMA ?

IN THE DARK OF NEXT MORNING AT 0245 LT NAGASHIMA SABURO FLEW HIS MAVIS BACK TO TRUK TO COLLECT MORE SUPPLIES AND MEN. A FEW HOURS LATER AT DAWN, NEMOTO CLIMBED THE ISLAND'S HILL SPINE WHICH ROSE A MODEST 50 FEET ABOVE SEA LEVEL. FROM HERE HE SURVEYED HIS NEW SURROUNDS, & ESTIMATED THAT THE ISLAND'S WIDTH WAS ABOUT 50 METRES AND ABOUT TWO KILOMETRES LONG. HE WAS DEAD ACCURATE! THE ISLAND IS THE LARGEST IN THE THE ATOLL'S EXPANSIVE CIRCULAR ATOLL. NAGASHIMA RETURNED FROM TRUK THAT SAME AFTERNOON AT 1552. FOR HIM IT HAD BEEN A PARTICULALRY LONG DAY.

AGAIN, THE PESKY RAAF IS ABOUT TO FEATURE HEAVILY IN NEMOTO'S LIFE, BOMBING THE WEE ISLAND WITH ITS HUDSONS. THIS IS AN OPPORTUNE JUNCTURE TO REMIND READERS THAT THE AUSTRALIANS & JAPANESE HAD BEEN FRIENDS IN THE GREAT WAR, ONLY TWO DECADES PRIOR, PARTICULARLY THEIR NAVIES. BELOW PHOTO WAS TAKEN IN 1916 OF A JAPANESE SAILOR SECONDED TO AN AUSTRALIAN WARSHIP DURING THAT WAR.

HARDSHIPS!
on Kapingamarangi

- little fresh water
- no saki
- no Wensleydale

AUSTRALIA
JAPAN

BEAUT MATES!

THAT 9 JANUARY MORNING, THE ATOLL DETACHMENT RECEIVED A MESSAGE OF ENCOURAGEMENT FROM COMMANDER OF THE FOURTH FLEET, VICE-ADMIRAL INOUE SHIGEYOSHI. THIS WELL-TRAVELLED OFFICER SHOWCASED WORDLY CREDENTIALS. HE HAD EVEN ATTENDED THE 1911 CORONATION OF KING GEORGE V IN LONDON!

WELL DONE COMRADES !

MEANWHILE THE UNIDENTIFIED PETTY OFFICER IN CHARGE OF THE FLOATPLANES RETURNED TO TRUK ON NAGASHIMA'S MAVIS THAT MORNING HANDING NEMOTO COMMANDMENT OF THE DETACHMENT. NEMOTO WROTE THAT EVENING *"I HAVE TO LOOK AFTER EVERYBODY NOW"*.

A ROBUST MESSAGE OF ENCOURAGEMENT TO BOOST THE LADS' MORALE

PROMOTION!

THIS IS WHERE THE STORY REALLY STARTS TO ACCELERATE. THUS FAR WE HAVE INTRODUCED DEANNA DURBIN (EXPLANE-ATION OF WHY SOON FORTHCOMING), PORCO ROSSO (THE GREATEST AVIATION ANIMATION EVER MADE), AND, *INTER ALIA*, THE FACT THAT THE ISLAND'S INTREPID AVIATORS ON THE ISLAND HAD NO WENSLEYDALE CHEESE.

NOW ITS TIME TO ADD ANOTHER UNIQUE FEATURE; A COCONUT DOLL. HOWEVER, LIKE DEANNA DURBIN YOU WILL HAVE TO WAIT TO SEE WHY IT FEATURES. BE ASSURED IT IS BOTH IMPORTANT AND INTEGRAL TO THE FAST-PACED UNFOLDING NARRATIVE.

I WONDER WHAT THE ISLAND PARADISE IS GUNNA BE LIKE?

MEANWHILE. . . REINFORCEMENTS ARE ON THE WAY !

A shotai (flight) of three Jakes arrives from 17 Naval Air Group

ON MORNING OF 12 JANUARY '41 THREE JAKES HEAD FOR KAPINGAMARANGI FROM TRUK. WELL BEFORE THESE REINFORCEMENTS ARRIVE, NEMOTO GETS UP AT 0300 AND LEADS THE FIRST PATROL AN HOUR LATER.

THE ATOLL WAS OFTEN COVERED BY LIGHT CUMULUS

THE TRIO LET DOWN OVER THE ATOLL AT 1430 HOURS, AFTER A THREE-HOUR FLIGHT. WITH THE DETACHMENT NOW TOTALLING SEVEN FLOATPLANES, NEMOTO CONTINUES A REGIME OF LONG-RANGE PATROLS ALWAYS LEAVING EARLY MORNING.

"A HIERARCHICAL TERM"

Warrant Officer

飛曹長
hisocho

35

THAT EVENING NEMOTO WROTE, "THREE HOURS PER PATROL BUT I BEGAN TO FEEL SLIGHTLY BORED TOWARDS THE END. I SANG IN A LOUD VOICE ALTHOUGH IT WAS DROWNED OUT BY ENGINE ROAR. I FORGOT TO BRING MY MIRROR AND WONDERED HOW I LOOKED. I FELT A BIT LONELY".
BUT HE DOES NOT MENTION WHAT HE WAS SINGING.

PERHAPS IT WAS 'RABAURU KOUTA' ?

THE MAIN ISLAND ON KAPINGAMARANGI ATOLL USED AS THE FLOATPLANE BASE

THE SIGNIFICANCE OF 'RABAURU KOUTA' TO BE EXPLAINED LATER

IT HAD BEEN QUIET FOR SEVERAL DAYS WHEN ON 15 JANUARY NEMOTO WROTE, *"SEVERAL NATIVES ARRIVED IN CANOES, COMPLAINING THEIR LIVES HAVE BEEN DISTURBED BY HAVING TO WORK FOR IMPERIAL JAPAN. THEY CAN OF COURSE, LIVE WITHOUT WORKING DUE TO THE ABUNDANT RESOURCES HERE. IT SEEMS THE GREATER ASIA WAR IS CAUSING THEM INCONVENIENCE. IT CANNOT BE HELPED HOWEVER AS WE NEED THEIR HELP."*

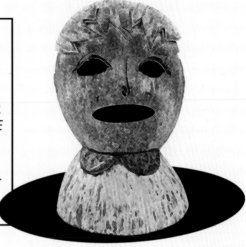

TIME TO INTRODUCE THE COCONUT DOLL, AS PROMISED. ON 15 JANUARY NEMOTO WROTE, *"WHEN THE COMMANDER OF 17 NAVAL AIR GROUP VISITED AT THE END OF LAST YEAR* **[HIKOTAICHO LT-COMMANDER SUGAWARA HIDEO 菅原英雄 EARLIER CITED),** *A COMMEMORATION DOLL WAS PLACED ON THE SLIPWAY, MADE FROM AN UPTURNED COCONUT TREE. THE RESULT WAS TWO PLANES BURNED, SEVERAL LIVES LOST, AND SEVERAL PETROL TANKS DESTROYED. A VERY GREAT LOSS. OF COURSE, AND THE DOLL WAS SOON REMOVED . . . "*

A FEW DAYS OF PEACE WAS INTERUPTED WHEN ON 17 JANUARY, JUST AFTER LUNCH, TWO HUDSONS BOMBED KOEI MARU, THEN DESCENDED TO STRAFE HER. THIS TIME TWO PETES AND ONE JAKE SCRAMBLED. THE JAKE WAS FLOWN BY WO ISHIKAWA YOSHIO AND THE FIRST PETE BY FPO2c TAGUCHI YU'URO. OUR HERO NEMOTO CLAMBERED INTO THE SECOND PETE, TAIL CODE R-16, IN SUCH A HURRY THAT THERE WAS INSUFFICIENT TIME TO BOARD HIS GUNNER/ OBSERVER. HE WROTE, *"I BOARDED #16 ALONE WITHOUT CAP OR GLOVES, & CHASED THE ENEMY BUT THEY ESCAPED QUICKLY INTO CLOUD. I LANDED AFTER A FURTHER 20-MINUTE PATROL."*

NEXT DAY THE HUDSONS SWEPT IN AND BOMBED PETE R-16 MOORED CLOSELY OFFSHORE NEAR THE RAMP. ANOTHER PETE & JAKE CLIMBED TO 3000 METRES TO UNSUCCESFULLY PERSUE THE FLEEING RAAF FELLOWS, FLOWN BY HORITA YOSHITAKA & FPO1c DAIWA TOKUZO.

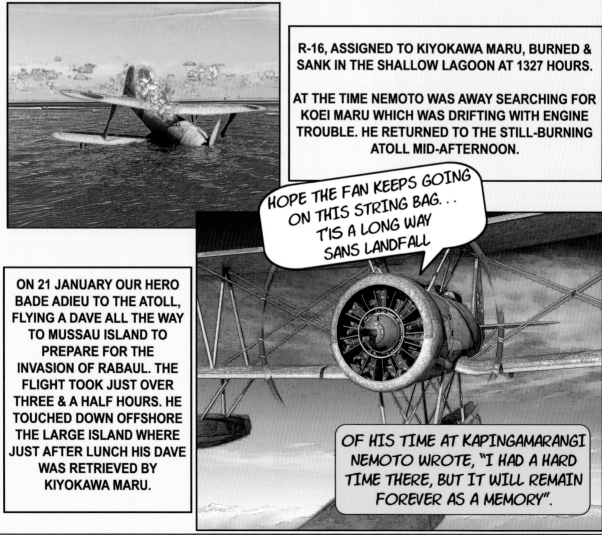

R-16, ASSIGNED TO KIYOKAWA MARU, BURNED & SANK IN THE SHALLOW LAGOON AT 1327 HOURS.

AT THE TIME NEMOTO WAS AWAY SEARCHING FOR KOEI MARU WHICH WAS DRIFTING WITH ENGINE TROUBLE. HE RETURNED TO THE STILL-BURNING ATOLL MID-AFTERNOON.

ON 21 JANUARY OUR HERO BADE ADIEU TO THE ATOLL, FLYING A DAVE ALL THE WAY TO MUSSAU ISLAND TO PREPARE FOR THE INVASION OF RABAUL. THE FLIGHT TOOK JUST OVER THREE & A HALF HOURS. HE TOUCHED DOWN OFFSHORE THE LARGE ISLAND WHERE JUST AFTER LUNCH HIS DAVE WAS RETRIEVED BY KIYOKAWA MARU.

OF HIS TIME AT KAPINGAMARANGI NEMOTO WROTE, "I HAD A HARD TIME THERE, BUT IT WILL REMAIN FOREVER AS A MEMORY".

ラバウル
(Katakana for Rabaul)

MEANWHILE, RAAF NO. 24 SQUADRON CHAPPIES ENJOYED A PEACEFUL LIFESTYLE IN PRE-WAR RABAUL, OPERATING WIRRAWAY 'FIGHTERS' ALONGSIDE HUDSONS. THE AGREEABLE ENVIRONS OFFERED NICE GOLF COURSE TOO (SEE BELOW), WITH GLORIOUS SUNSETS.

PORT MORESBY-BASED CATALINA FLYING BOATS FROM RAAF NOS 11 AND 20 SQUADRONS WOULD OFTEN VISIT, BRINGING SUPPLIES OF MAIL, GOODIES & WHISKEY. THEY WERE WELCOME VISITORS

WHEN THE JAPANESE FINALLY SEIZED RABAUL, THE INCUMBENT AUSTRALIANS WERE UNDERSTANDABLY VERY UNHAPPY. IT STEELED THEIR RESOLVE TO FIGHT THE JAPANESE

EASE HER OFF AT 7,000. I HEAR DRINKS ARE ON TONIGHT AT THE CLUB

HOLD HER STEADY WHILE I REPAIR BACKSTAGE FOR A COFFEE

New Guinea Club Rabaul

THIS IS THE CLUB TO WHICH THE CATALINA DUDE REFERS - THE NEW GUINEA CLUB WHICH WAS THE SOCIAL CENTRE OF RABAUL. INDEED, IT STILL EXISTS TODAY AS A NOSTALGIC REMINDER OF A BYGONE ERA. THE COSMOPOLITAN HOTEL WAS ALSO POPULAR, RUN BY MR MIDDLETON. ON THE TOWN'S SMALL TELEPHONE EXCHANGE 192 WAS THE NUMBER FOR THE COSMOPOLITAN. RABAUL BOASTED SEVERAL FORD SEDANS, SEEN ABOVE. THESE WERE LATER USED BY THE JAPANESE FOR VIP TRANSPORTATION. CHECK OUT THE BELOW PHOTO OF AUSTRALIAN SOLDIERS MARCHING PAST THE COSMOPOLITAN HOTEL IN LATE 1939.

ラバウル小唄

MENTIONED PREVIOUSLY, THE JAPANESE SONG 'RABUARU KOUTA' ('RABAUL DITTY') BECAME FAMOUS IN JAPAN POST-WAR, SUNG BY POPULAR SINGERS. IT REMAINED A CONNECTOR OF CULTURE BETWEEN THE TOLAI LOCALS & JAPANESE LONG AFTER THEY LEFT RABAUL. SOME VERSES ARE EVEN WRITTEN IN TOLAI.THE SONG REFLECTS THE TIME WHEN JAPAN SEEMED TO BE AN UNSTOPPABLE FORCE IN THE SOUTH PACIFIC. TO THE LEFT IS HOW 'RABAURU KOUTA' IS WRITTEN IN JAPANESE.

MEANWHILE LIFE WENT ON AS NORMAL IN RABAUL, HOWEVER RUMOURS & CONCERNS ABOUT A POSSIBLE INVASION INCREASED DAILY.

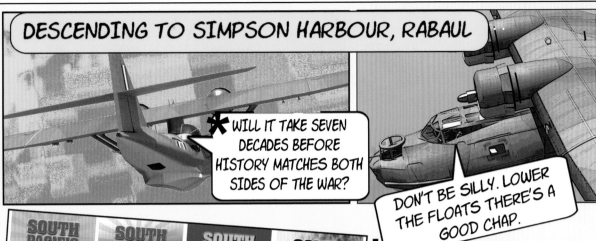

DESCENDING TO SIMPSON HARBOUR, RABAUL

* WILL IT TAKE SEVEN DECADES BEFORE HISTORY MATCHES BOTH SIDES OF THE WAR?

DON'T BE SILLY. LOWER THE FLOATS THERE'S A GOOD CHAP.

* IN FACT NO-ONE PROPERLY MATCHED ALLIED AGAINST JAPANESE RECORDS UNTIL 2018 WHEN FOUR VOLUMES OF 'SOUTH PACIFIC AIR WAR' BY AVONMORE BOOKS (AUSTRALIA) WAS THE FIRST SERIES TO BREAK THE CYCLE OF ONE-SIDED HISTORY.

Rabaul's First Air Raid . . .

ONLY ONE DAY AFTER PEARL HARBOR, NERVOUS EYES AT RABAUL OBSERVED A LUMBERING MAVIS FLYING BOAT HIGH OVERHEAD. THE TOWN'S FIRST AIR-RAID FELL ON 4 JANUARY 1942 CONDUCTED BY 16 NELL BOMBERS OF CHITOSE NAVAL AIR GROUP FROM TRUK. THEY APPROACHED OVERHEAD TABAR ISLAND WHERE PLANTATION MANAGER CORNELIUS PAGE RADIOED A WARNING. AN AUSTRALIAN AA BATTERY FIRED AT THEM, AND TWO RAAF WIRRAWAYS TOOK OFF TOO. THE AA ROUNDS FELL SHORT & CAPTAIN SELBY'S MEN BECAME THE FIRST AUSTRALIANS IN COMBAT ON AUSTRALIAN TERRITORY. SELBY RECOUNTED HOW THE BOMBS FELL NEAR LAKUNAI AIRFIELD, *"THE EARTH AT THE FAR END OF THE AERODROME LEAPT & DANCED IN A HUGE SWIRLING COLUMN AS A SALVO OF BOMBS FELL ACROSS IT."*

KIYOKAWA MARU'S FLOATPLANES WERE STATIONED AT MUSSAU ISLAND SO THEY COULD PATROL OVERHEAD THE APPROACHING MERCHANTMEN IN RABAUL'S INVASION FLEET. ON 22 JANUARY, THE DAY BEFORE THE INVASION, DAVE R-21 DISAPPEARED WITH PILOT FPO1c TERAMO KAZUO & OBSERVER/ GUNNER FPO2c KAJIYAMA SHIN. IT TURNED OUT THEY OUTLANDED IN BAD WEATHER, AND WERE LATER RETURNED SAFELY TO THE SHIP.

THROUGHOUT LATE 1941 INCREASING CONCERN BY THE GOOD CITIZENS OF RABAUL HAD SEEN MUCH COMMUNITY DISCUSSION. ONE VENUE WHERE THE THE MATTER AIRED WAS THE COMMONWEALTH BANK ON MANGO AVENUE, PICTURED ABOVE. THIS STURDY COLONIAL BUILDING WOULD LATER BECOME A STAFF HEADQUARTERS FOR THE IJN. THE POSSIBLE INVASION OF THE TOWN WAS ALSO A SOURCE OF CONSTANT SPECULATION & RUMOUR.

AND, ASIDE FROM ITS ACTIVE (AND PICTURESQUE) VOLCANOES, RABAUL WAS ALSO THE HOME OF RAAF NO. 24 SQUADRON AS KEENLY DEMONSTRATED SO FAR.

18 DECEMBER 1941 – A PAIR OF SNOOPERS HEAD FOR RABAUL

THESE DUDES ARE FROM TRUK, MAKING SURE RABAUL IS NOT BEING REINFORCED.

PASSING OVER NEW IRELAND REEFS

ON 18 DECEMBER SQN-LDR LEREW DIVIDED HIS WIRRAWAYS INTO TWO GROUPS, RETAINING 'B' FLIGHT AT VUNAKANAU AND MOVING 'A' FLIGHT TO LAKUNAI WHERE THE AIRCRAFT WERE DISPERSED AMONG COCONUT TREES TO HELP CONCEAL THEM. THAT SAME DAY TWO YOKOHAMA NAVAL AIR GROUP MAVIS APPEARED OVER RABAUL.

"CAN'T SEE ANY BAD BUGGERS"

"LOOK LIVELY LADS, I CAN SEE TWO BAD BOYS AHEAD"

THESE WIRRAS ALSO CARRIED A REAR GUNNER

FOUR WIRRAWAYS SCRAMBLED BUT WERE UNABLE TO CATCH THE SNOOPERS *"OWING TO LACK OF SPEED"*. THEY MUCH LAMENTED A SITUATION WHEREBY THEIR SO-CALLED "FIGHTERS" COULD NEITHER CATCH NOR OVERTAKE THE LUMBERING FLYING BOATS.

JUDAS PRIEST, SHE WON'T GO ANY DAMNED FASTER !

...EVEN WITH THE F#@#$ THROTTLE FIREWALLED !

Check out these unusual wing roundels

THE RAAF WIRRAWAYS COULD BARELY CLIMB TO MEET ATTACKERS, LET ALONE KEEP UP WITH THEM. DESIGNED AS TRAINERS YET THEY WERE DEPLOYED TO RABAUL AS FIGHTERS.

SAD!

TALLY HO MY BLOODY FOOT NOT A (EXPLETIVE DELETED) SHOT FIRED.

Heading back to Lakunai . . .

HOW TO EXPLAIN MY F#+^% JOYFLIGHT TO THE WINGCO ?

24 RAAF SQUADRON BADGE

SPITFIRE SHE AIN'T I'M OUTA HERE

A20-103

THIS CROSS IS A JAPANESE INTRUDER

44

MEANWHILE IN AUSTRALIA, AND WHILE NEMOTO WAS ON HIS WAY TO KAPINGAMARANGI IN THE MAVIS, THERE WAS WELL-FOUNDED CONCERN OVER THE JAPANESE BUILD-UP AT TRUK, AS ANY THREAT TO RABAUL WOULD EMANATE FROM HERE. STEMMING FROM THESE CONCERNS, THE GALLANT LADS IN THE RAAF HAD A RETALIATORY AND CUNNING PLAN . . .

THE JIG IS UP !

DATELINE: Kavieng on New Britain 0544 Hours 9 January 1942

A VISUAL RECONNAISSANCE OF TRUK WAS URGENTLY NEEDED, AND TWO LONG-RANGE HUDSON MARK IVs WERE CHOSEN FOR THE TASK, EQUIPPED WITH TWO EXTRA 105-GALLON FUSELAGE FUEL TANKS. FLYING OFFICER YEOWART OF RAAF NO. 6 SQUADRON DEPARTED KAVIENG AT 0544 HOURS ON 9 JANUARY 1942. FOUR AND A HALF HOURS LATER, HIS HUDSON EMERGED FROM A SQUALL DIRECTLY OVERHEAD TRUK ATOLL WHERE THEY COUNTED A DOZEN DESTROYERS AND LIGHT CRUISERS – THIS WAS THE FOURTH FLEET BACK FROM WAKE. ALSO MOORED IN THE HARBOUR WERE EIGHT SILVER FOUR-ENGINED FLYING BOATS AND NUMEROUS FLOATPLANES. THE JIG WAS UP !

HURRY UP AND GET THOSE PHOTOS SERGEANT!

JUDAS PRIEST ! FIGHTERS ARE SCRAMBLING BELOW !

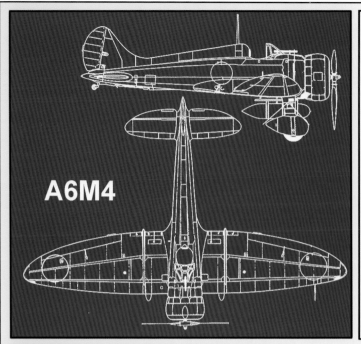

A6M4

CAN YOU GUESS WHICH TYPE OF FIGHTERS WERE ON CLIMB TO CONFRONT THE BRAVE HUDSON LADS

?

SEE THE INSTRUMENT PANEL BELOW, CLEARLY NOT THAT OF A ZERO!

THE A5M4 WAS AN ANTIQUATED MONOPLANE WHICH HAD SERVED IN CHINA. IT WAS MORE SUITABLE AS A GENTLEMAN'S SPORTS AIRCRAFT THAN A FIGHTER, CERTAINLY FOR THE VAST CHALLENGES OF THE PACIFIC.

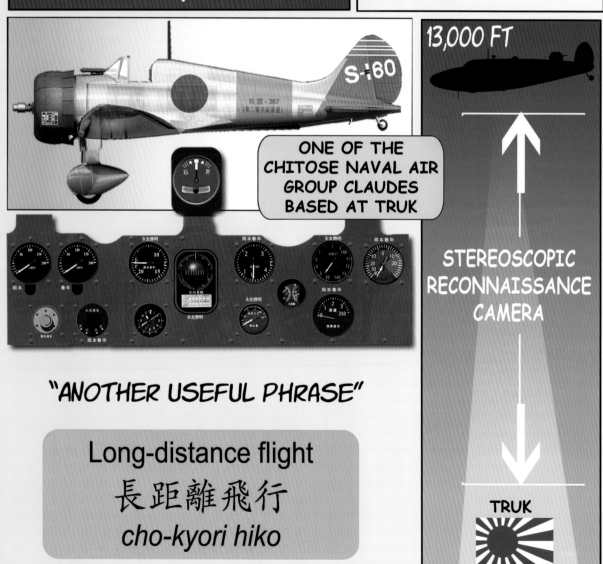

S-160

ONE OF THE CHITOSE NAVAL AIR GROUP CLAUDES BASED AT TRUK

13,000 FT

STEREOSCOPIC RECONNAISSANCE CAMERA

TRUK

"ANOTHER USEFUL PHRASE"

Long-distance flight

長距離飛行

cho-kyori hiko

THE INTERCEPTORS WERE THE SAME CLAUDE FIGHTERS FROM CHITOSE NAVAL AIR GROUP ON WHICH NEMOTO AND HIS PALS HAD RECENTLY BEEN TRAINING AT TRUK.

NIIICE POLISHED METAL

CHITOSE NAVAL AIR GROUP HEROS RISE TO THE OCCASION

A SECOND PHOTGRAPHIC RUN AT 13,000 FT COST AN EXTRA 25 MINUTES OVER TARGET, GIVING ENOUGH TIME FOR THE CLAUDES TO CLIMB TO ALTITUDE. YEOWART'S TURRET GUNNER GAVE THE LEAD FIGHTER A LONG BURST, THEN THE HUDSON DIVED INTO A RAIN SQUALL TO ESCAPE. YEOWART RECOVERED AT SEA-LEVEL, THEN REFUELLED AT KAVIENG BEFORE RETURNING TO RABAUL. NEXT MORNING HIS HUDSON DELIVERED THE FILM TO TOWNSVILLE WHERE INTELLIGENCE CHAPPIES POURED OVER THE PHOTOS.

RAT TAT TAT TAT TAT

GET US OUTA HERE SIR! I CAN'T HOLD THEM OFF!

REFRESH YOUR RECOLLECTION OF THIS PAGE

PLEASE RECALL WHEN NEMOTO LEFT KAPINGAMARANGI AS THE CHRONOLOGY GETS MORE COMPLICATED

YOU WILL RECALL THAT ON 21 JANUARY NEMOTO LEFT KAPINGAMARANGI FOR THE LAST TIME, FLYING HIS DAVE ALL THE WAY TO MUSSAU ISLAND WHERE HE REJOINED KIYOKAWA MARU TO PREPARE FOR THE INVASION OF RABAUL.

AT THIS JUNCTURE WE FAREWELL NO. 17 NAVAL AIR GROUP, NOW WIDELY SCATTERED OVER THE PACIFIC. THEY PLAY NO ROLE IN THE INVASION OF RABAUL; THEIR TWO DAVES ARE DETACHED AT KWAJALEIN, THEIR JAKES ARE SERVING ABOARD AUXILIARY CRUISERS KONGO MARU & KINRYU MARU, & THEIR SIX PETES REMAIN AT KAPINGAMARANGI.

SOUTH PACIFIC AIR WAR

VOLUME ONE

THE FALL OF RABAUL
DECEMBER 1941 TO MARCH 1942

INVASION OF RABAUL - READ ABOUT IT HERE!

THE OCCUPATION OF RABAUL ON 23 JANUARY 1942 WAS A BTO (BIG-TIME OPERATION) PRECEDED BY NUMEROUS CARRIER STRIKES. NEMOTO AWOKE AT 0330 TO PATROL THE INVASION FLOTILLA BUT DID NOT TAKE OFF DUE TO HEAVY RAIN. VOLUME ONE OF 'SOUTH PACIFIC AIR WAR' IS THE ONLY PUBLICATION TO ALIGN THE TWO SIDES OF THE AIR WAR.

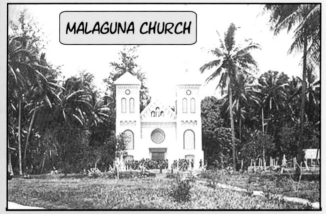

MALAGUNA CHURCH

LATER THAT EVENING ABOARD THE SHIP NEMOTO CAME DOWN WITH HIGH FEVER. HE RESTED THE NEXT DAY WITH A PERSISTENT HIGH TEMPERATURE OF 37.2 CELCIUS. HE RECOVERED AND ON 28 JANUARY MOVED ASHORE WHERE THE SHIP'S PILOTS TOOK UP ACCOMMODATION IN A SCHOOL HOUSE ADJACENT TO THE MALAGUNA CHURCH. IT WAS DESTROYED BY ALLIED BOMBING IN 1943.

NEMOTO WRITES "RABAUL IS A DEAD PLACE WITH NAVY PERSONNEL + NATIVES WANDERING AROUND. ONE MUST NOT LOSE A WAR".

NORWEIGAN SHIP SS HERSTEIN BURNS FOR DAYS IN THE HARBOUR

NEMOTO IN THE GROUNDS OF MALAGUNA CHURCH, RABAUL

BY 6 FEBRUARY NEMOTO IS FULLY-RECOVERED, AND DISCOVERS HE HAD BEEN AFFLICTED WITH DENGUE FEVER. LAND-BASED FIGHTERS SOON ARRIVE AT RABAUL, SO INSTEAD OF FLYING LOCAL PATROLS, THE SHIP'S FLOATPLANES SWITCH TO LONG-RANGE PATROLS 300 MILES OUT TO SEA. THE NEWLY-ARRIVED FIGHTERS ARE MODEL 21 ZEROS ADOPTED INTO NO. 4 NAVAL AIR GROUP UPON ARRIVAL AT RABAUL, A COMBINED BOMBER/ FIGHTER UNIT CREATED SPECIALLY FOR THE 'SOUTH SEAS'. THE ZEROS ARE BASED AT LAKUNAI AIRFIELD NEAR THE OLD AUSTRALIAN GOLF COURSE, NOT FAR FROM THE NEW GUINEA CLUB.

"AN INDISPENSIBLE CODE"

Location Code RRF

ガスマタ

Gasmata

LAND-BASED ZEROS NOW OPERATE FROM LAKUNAI

A6M2 ZERO TAIL F-115 FLOWN BY LT OKAMOTO HARUTOSHI COMMANDER OF NO. 4 NAVAL AIR GROUP FIGHTER WING

THE UNIT BECOMES KNOWN AROUND RABAUL AS THE 'OKAMOTO BUTAI'

F-115

OKAMOTO WAS RECALLED TO JAPAN IN APRIL 1942, HOWEVER HE RETURNED TO RABAUL IN LATE 1943 TO TAKE UP THE POSITION OF BUNTAICHO OF 253 NAVAL AIR GROUP, BUT NOW BACK TO NEMOTO'S CRACKING TALE . . .

FITNESS REPORT
WO NEMOTO Kumesako

"ANOTHER USEFUL PHRASE"

'Surumi' in Katakana
スルミ

ON 6 FEBRUARY NEMOTO TURNS HIS MIND TO MORE PROSAIC MATTERS. HE IS INTERVIEWED AT A 'PROMOTION MEETING' ASHORE. NORMALLY PROMOTION ASPIRANTS ARE SUBJECT TO EXAMINATIONS, BUT THESE HAVE BEEN WAIVED UNDER WARTIME CONDITIONS. PROMOTIONS WILL BE ANNOUNCED ON 1 APRIL 42, HOWEVER HE STILL HAS TO SUBMIT A WRITTEN APPLICATION.

THE NEXT DAY THE SHIP'S FLOATPLANES ARE RECOVERED BY KIYOKAWA MARU, ORDERED TO ASSIST THE INVASION OF GASMATA, ALSO REFERRED TO BY THE JAPANESE AS 'SURUMI'.

NEMOTO SPENDS THAT AFTERNOON IN HIS CABIN COMPLETING HIS PROMOTION APPLICATION. NOW WE TURN TO A NEW CHAPTER IN OUR HERO'S LIFE.

INVASION OF SURUMI (GASMATA)

PATROLS THROUGHOUT THE OPERATION OF ABOUT THREE HOURS EACH.

ON 9 FEBRUARY KIYOKAWA MARU ANCHORED IN MONTAGU BAY, ABOUT 45 MILES EAST OF SURUMI. THAT MORNING NEMOTO CATAPAULTED AT 0500 HOURS FOR AN EXTENDED PATROL DURING WHICH HE OBSERVED IJN PIONEER UNITS ASHORE UNDERTAKING REPAIR WORK. WITH THE INVASION COMPLETE, THE SHIP'S PILOTS WERE TOLD THAT AS SOON AS LAND-BASED FIGHTERS ARRIVED, THE SHIP WOULD RETURN TO RABAUL. NEMOTO WROTE THAT EVENING,

"I WATCHED THE NATIVES THROUGH THE BINOCULARS ON THE BRIDGE. I WAS SURPRISED TO SEE SO MANY CHILDREN. MEN WEAR RED CLOTHES AROUND THEIR WAIST AND THE WOMEN WEAR GRASS SKIRTS."

ON 11 FEBRUARY NEMOTO CATAPAULTED AT 0415 HOURS IN A DAVE. HE WAS INCREASINGLY DESPONDENT AT THE DAVE'S LACK OF HORSEPOWER AND FIREPOWER, LARGELY DERVIED FROM AN UNSATISFACTORY INCIDENT THE DAY PREVIOUS ...

ON THE DAY PREVIOUS OF 10 FEBRUARY HIS OLD RAAF FRIENDS, THE RAAF 24 SQUADRON HUDSONS, PAID GASMATA A COURTESY CALL AT MIDDAY. BOOTED OUT OF RABAUL BUT NOW BASED AT PORT MORESBY, FOUR HUDSONS WERE HELL-BENT ON REVENGE FOR THE LOSS OF RABAUL. NEMOTO WAS ALREADY AIRBORNE ON PATROL, & HIS OBSERVER FIRED HIS PISTOL AT THEM [EXCLAMATION], BUT FOR NOUGHT. HE WROTE THAT EVENING THAT *"MY MOUNT PROVED TOO WEAK IN HORSEPOWER AND CONSEQUENTLY I HAD NO CHANCE TO FIRE MY FIXED GUNS"*.

FINALLY WE CAN REVEAL WHY HOLLYWOOD HEART-THROB DEANNA DURBIN FEATURES IN THIS THRILLING ADVENTURE OF THE PACIFIC SEAS & AIR. SEE BELOW WHAT NEMOTO PENNED THAT EVENING.

"I PLACED A PHOTO OF DEANNA DURBIN IN MY ROOM TODAY. SHE HAS BEAUTIFUL EYES. I WILL CHANGE IT TO PHOTOS OF MY WIFE + CHILDREN WHEN THEY REACH ME. THERE IS NO MAIL BOAT HERE HOWEVER AND THEREFORE NO CONSOLATION. SEA + SKY ARE THE ONLY THINGS ONE CAN SEE IN THE DISTANCE. I HOPE MY FAMILY IS IN GOOD HEALTH, MEANWHILE ALL THE SHIP'S COMPLEMENT ARE IN HIGH SPIRITS."

Aircraft fabric

飛行機用羽布

hikoki yo hafu

"TERMINOLOGY GALORE"

NO. 4 NAVAL AIR GROUP
CLAUDES GO TO WORK

ON 11 FEBRUARY 1942, TWO DETACHMENTS OF CLAUDES LEFT RABAUL BOUND FOR GASMATA. THE FIRST TRIO COMPRISED FPO3c ISHIKAWA KIYOJI, FLYER1c TANJI JUFUKU & FPO2c MIYA UN'ICHI WHICH ARRIVED FIRST WITHOUT INCIDENT. FOUR MORE FOLLOWED LED BY FPO1c YOSHINO SATOSHI, WHICH APPROACHED SURUMI MID-AFTERNOON. BY COINCIDENCE THEY ARRIVED JUST AS THREE RAAF HUDSONS ATTACKED AT LOW LEVEL. THESE WERE LED BY NEMOTO'S OLD FRIEND SQUADARON LEADER JOHN LEREW FLYING A16-91. THE AUSTRALIANS BOMBED SHIPS IN THE HARBOUR.

YOSHINO'S CLAUDES FOUGHT THE HUDSONS PERSISTENTLY AND CLAIMED ALL THREE. IN FACT, THE JAPANESE FIGHTERS SHOT DOWN TWO, EXPENDING 2,800 ROUNDS. MERCHANTMAN KINRYU MARU SUSTAINED A DIRECT HIT WHICH KILLED A DOZEN SAILORS AND BADLY INJURED MANY MORE. KOZUI MARU WAS LIKEWISE BLASTED BY THREE BOMBS.

THESE RUPTURED THE HULL CAUSING LIMITED FLOODING.
EMERGENCY REPAIRS WERE SOON EFFECTED.

THE JUNGLE FOOTHILLS
BEHIND GASMATA

ANCHORED OFF THE 'BEEHIVES' IN SIMPSON HARBOUR

MEANWHILE, HER JOB DONE, THAT EVENING KIYOKAWA MARU PULLED ANCHOR AND RETURNED TO RABAUL WHERE SHE ARRIVED MORNING OF 13 FEBRUARY. THE TENDER HAD LUCKILY ESCAPED THE HUDSON ATTACK AS IT HAD BEEN ANCHORED IN MONTAGU BAY, A FAIR WAY FROM THE ACTION. NOW THAT LAND-BASED FIGHTERS HAD ARRIVED AT SURUMI THE SHIP'S FLOATPLANES WERE NO LONGER NEEDED THERE.

FOR THE NEXT FEW DAYS NEMOTO + HIS COMRADES FLY UNEVENTFUL DAILY PATROLS OVER RABAUL

ROAD TO RABAUL

OVERHEAD LAKUNAI AIRFIELD

ON 15 FEBRUARY NEMOTO RECORDS THAT HE HAS BEEN BATHING DAILY IN HOT WATER, *"BECAUSE SEAWATER IS MIXED WITH THE HOT SPRING I HAVE TO WASH IN FRESH WATER AFTERWARDS. LATELY IT HAS BEEN COOL IN THE BARRACKS ALTHOUGH HOT DURING THE DAY. I WILL NOT TRY TO EXERT MYSELF. EVERYTHING MUST BE BASED FOR THE LONG TERM"*.

OPPOSITE IS A PHOTO OF THE AUTHOR IN 2018 WITH A FRIENDLY GUIDE TAKEN AT THE SITE OF THESE HOT SPRINGS, ON THE SHORELINE JUST TO THE NORTH OF LAKUNAI AIRFIELD. THE HOT SPRINGS ARE ABOUT 20 METRES TO THE LEFT OF THIS PHOTO.

'THE MOTHER' VOLCANO

CALM BEFORE THE STORM. . .
QUIET DAYS AT RABAUL.

ON 20 FEBRUARY NEMOTO WROTE, "*THE WAR IS PROGRESSING RAPIDLY, ON 18 FEBRUARY WE CAPTURED SINGAPORE. IT WILL NOT BE LONG NOW UNTIL WE CHASE BRITAIN AND AMERICA FROM THE GREATER ASIA CO-PROSPERITY SPHERE. OUR ENEMY IS THE OLD BRITISH EMPIRE.*"

A G4M1 BETTY BOMBER
OF NO. 4 NAVAL AIR GROUP

HOWEVER THAT SAME AFTERNOON IJN FORCES AT RABAUL WERE SHOCKED TO LEARN OF THE LOSS OF THIRTEEN BETTYS WHICH HAD UNSUCCESSFULLY ATTACKED USN CARRIER LEXINGTON, A LONG WAY OUT TO SEA FROM RABAUL. ANOTHER TWO DITCHED DUE TO COMBAT DAMAGE. TWO MAVIS FLYING BOATS WERE ALSO SHOT DOWN, AND ANOTHER DISAPPEARED IN BAD WEATHER. KIYOKAWA MARU SUFFERED THE LAST LOSS OF THE DAY WHEN A JAKE FLOWN BY PILOT MATSUE DISAPPEARED THAT AFTERNOON WHILE SEARCHING FOR LEXINGTON.

IJN Aircraft losses
20 February 1942

15   1   3

SOMEWHERE OVER NEW IRELAND IN DARK STORY WEATHER + WITHOUT NAVIGATION AIDS

JUMPIN' FUJI, CAN'T SEE A DOGGONE THING

THE END OF MATSUE'S CREW

REQUESTING BEARINGS OVER, OVER, OVER

THE SHIP'S FLOATPLANES WERE PLACED ON STANDBY AT 1200 TO CONDUCT PATROLS TO FIND THE AMERICAN CARRIER. AT 2000 THAT NIGHT A KIYOKAWA MARU JAKE REQUESTED BEARINGS TO RETURN HOME, BUT THUNDERSTORMS PREVENTED ACCURATE BEARINGS BEING CALCULATED. THE SHIP'S RADIO OPERATOR ESTIMATED THAT THE STRICKEN JAKE WAS OVER NEW IRELAND AT 6,500 FEET ALTITUDE WHEN IT RAN OUT OF FUEL. PERHAPS ITS WRECKAGE IS STILL THERE

MIDNITE OVER RABAUL . . .

PACIFIC ADVERSARIES
Volume 2
IMPERIAL JAPANESE NAVY
vs The ALLIES
New Guinea & the Solomons 1942-1944

Michael John CLARINGBOULD

ON 26 FEBRUARY NEMOTO COMPLAINED ABOUT THE WAR'S DETERIORATING CIRCUMSTANCES, *"HOW LONG WILL THIS WAR LAST? MY COMRADES ARE ASCENDING TO HEAVEN ONE AFTER ANOTHER, FOR OUR SAKE AND FOR THE SAKE OF THE COUNTRY."* HE ALSO CONFIDED TO HIS DIARY ABOUT AN ENEMY RAID WHICH HAD OCCURRED MIDNIGHT THE PREVIOUS EVENING (ACTUALLY MADE BY RAAF CATALINAS) . OF COURSE, HE WOULD HAVE TAKEN HEART HAD HE KNOWN THAT THE FIRST JAPANESE ATTEMPT AT AERIAL NIGHT-FIGHTING WOULD BE DESCRIBED IN VOLUME 2 OF 'PACIFIC ADVERSARIES' PUBLISHED BY AVONMORE BOOKS, CITING RARE JAPANESE RECORDS FOR THE FIRST TIME!

RARE & FASCINATING HISTORY !

IMAGINE THE ADVERTISING CAMPAIGN HAD THE RAAF ENTERED
THE BUSINESS OF BREWING 'HUDSON' BEER FOR ITS OWN FLYBOYS . . .

HUDSON BEER

DOWNED ALL OVER NEW
GUINEA . . . JUST LIKE THE IJN

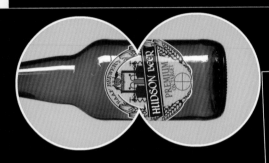

RELAX, ITS ONE OF OURS

IJN PILOTS DRINK
LEMONADE
MAKE IT A HUDSON

SAY "I WANT A HUDSON"

ZERO TOLERANCE !

DON'T LAND IN THE DRINK

AND, IMAGINE THE ADVERTISING CAMPAIGN HAD THE IJN HAD GOT INTO THE BUSINESS OF BREWING 'ANCHOR' BEER FOR ITS OWN HEROES ...

DISCERNING BUNTAICHO PREFER ANCHOR

TOO STRONG
For the Americans !

ENJOY ANCHOR !

WATCH OUT FOR HUDSONS ON YOUR THREE O'CLOCK

19:41
19:42
Anytime is a good time to drink ANCHOR

ST GEORGE'S POINT
NEW IRELAND

EARLY MORNING OF 26 FEBRUARY THE SHIP'S FLOATPLANES CO-ORDINATED AN OPERATION WITH AN IJN LANDING PARTY AND A PIONEER (CONSTRUCTION) UNIT. THE TASK WAS TO BUILD AN OBSERVATION POST ON ST GEORGE'S POINT ON NEW IRELAND, OPPOSITE RABAUL. THE POST WAS TO PROVIDE EARLY DETECTION OF APPROACHING ENEMY SHIPS & AIRCRAFT.

THAT EVENING THERE WAS AN OUTBREAK OF DIARRHOEA AT THE MALAGUNA BARRACKS. IT WAS BLAMED ON A STALE BATCH OF JAPANESE BEER DRUNK THE NIGHT BEFORE. THAT EVENING ALL KIYOKAWA MARU PERSONNEL WERE ORDERED TO RETURN TO THEIR SHIP. THIS TIME THEY WERE OFF AGAIN, AS PART OF A MAJOR MILITARY OPERATION, CODENAMED 'OPERATION SR'.

THE INVASION OF SALAMAUA + LAE WAS GIVEN THE NAME 'OPERATION SR' BY THE JAPANESE, NOT OPERATION 'SL'. TO UNDERSTAND WHY, READ BELOW.

'Lae' written 'Rae'
ラエ
Hence operation **SR** and not **SL**

ON EVENING OF 4 MARCH, NEMOTO AND HIS COMRADE PILOTS ATTENDED A LAVISH PARTY AT THE IJN HEADQUARTERS AT MALAGUNA, TO FAREWELL THOSE INVOLVED IN 'OPERATION SR'. NEMOTO CONFIDED TO HIS DIARY THE FOLLOWING DAY THAT AT THE FUNCTION HE HAD *"DRUNK SLIGHTLY TO EXCESS"*. KIYOKAWA MARU SAILED FROM RABAUL AT 1230 THE NEXT DAY, THEN OVER-NIGHTED AT LINDENHAFEN NEAR GASMATA ON EVENING OF 6 MARCH.

VEEERY EARLY ON 7 MARCH, JUST AFTER 0300, NEMOTO WASHED & HAD BREAKFAST. HE CATAPUALTED AT 0450 HOURS AND PATROLLED OVER MOWE HARBOUR 60 NAUTICAL MILES TO THE SOUTHWEST WHERE THE 'OPERATION SR' INVASION FLEET HAD ANCHORED. WHEN HE RETURNED TO THE SHIP HE TRIED TO SLEEP, BUT IT WAS ALREADY TOO HOT. HE NOTICED THAT HIS SWORD HAD BECOME SLIGHTLY RUSTY SO ASKED A PRIVATE FROM THE SHIP'S ENGINEERING BRANCH TO POLISH IT FOR HIM.

NEXT MORNING OF 8 MARCH NEMOTO TOOK THE SECOND PATROL & CATAPAULTED AT 0730 ON ANTI-SUBMARINE DUTY. THEN AT 0930 HE PATROLLED DIRECTLY BETWEEN LAE & SALAMAUA. FOR THE FIRST TIME HE ENCOUNTERED THE HAZARDOUS FLYING CONDITIONS PORTENDED BY THE MASSIVE GEOGRAPHY OF NEW GUINEA, OBSERVING, *"AT BOTH LOCATIONS THE CLOUD WAS LOW AND FLYING CONDITIONS WERE POOR"*. AT 1030 A HUDSON CAME OVER AND UNSUCCESSFULLY ATTACKED MOORED MERCHANTMAN YOKOHAMA MARU.

AT THIS JUNCTURE NEMOTO GIVES US A GLIMPSE INTO HIS BACKGROUND & INTERESTS. WHEN HE JOINED THE IJN HE HAD TO STUDY EITHER ENGLISH OR GERMAN. HE HE CHOSE THE LANGUAGE OF JAPAN'S ALLY.
SO, FOR RELAXATION ABOARD SHIP HE READS TOLSTOI'S 'WAR & PEACE' . HE DOES NOT SAY WHETHER IT IS IN JAPANESE OR GERMAN, BUT PROBABLY IN THE LATTER AS HE PROFESSES ENTHUSIASM TO MAINTAIN AND UPGRADE HIS GERMAN LANGUAGE PROFICIENCY.

'KRIEG UND FREIDEN' IS GERMAN FOR 'WAR AND PEACE'.

THE OPPOSITE BOOK IS NOT QUITE 'WAR AND PEACE' HOWEVER IT OUTLINES IN DETAIL THE MOMENTOUS DEVELOPMENTS IN THE AIR WAR ABOUT TO OCCUR. HERE YOU SEE THE WAR THROUGH NEMOTO'S EYES, HOWEVER IF YOU WANT THE BIGGER PICTURE THEN YOU MUST READ THIS BOOK (ALSO PUBLISHED BY AVONMORE BOOKS, AUSTRALIA).

IT IS GROUND-BREAKING FOR MANY REASONS, INCLUDING THE ALIGNMENT OF JAPANESE AND ALLIED RECORDS (WHICH MATCH NICELY).

FOR THE FIRST TIME THE INTREPID FLYERS ABOARD KIYOKAWA MARU ARE ABOUT TO MEET US NAVY PILOTS, SO HOLD ON. PARTS OF THE GRIPPING SAGA TO FOLLOW ALMOST FOLLOW 'WAR AND PEACE' !

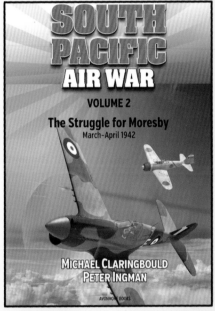

THE MIGHTY OWEN STANLEY RANGES

THE HEROIC NEMOTO IS ABOUT TO BECOME OF OF THE FEW DEFENDERS AGAINST THE MIGHTY ONSLAUGHT OF THE COMBINED AIRPOWER OF TWO USN AIRCRAFT CARRIERS . . .

KONGO MARU

TAKE THAT YOU N'ERE-DO'WELLS AND OVERALL BAD FELLOWS!

10 MARCH 1942 OFFSHORE LAE

A LONG, LONG WAY AWAY, ON THE OTHER SIDE OF NEW GUINEA AS DAWN APPROACHED ON 10 MARCH, AN ARMADA OF USN AIRCRAFT FROM CARRIERS LEXINGTON & YORKTOWN LAUNCHED EASTWARDS IN SMOOTH SEAS. AS THE CARRIERS STEAMED INTO WIND AT 25 KNOTS, LEXINGTON'S FIRST AIRCRAFT LAUNCHED AT 0749 HOURS, WITH YORKTOWN'S FOLLOWING SUIT 20 MINUTES LATER. A COMBINED FORCE OF 104 WILDCATS, DAUNTLESS AND DEVASTATORS HEADED THRU THE SUNSHINE GAP IN THE OWEN STANLEY MOUNTAINS, BOUND FOR TARGETS AROUND LAE & SALAMAUA. THIS VERILY WAS A MASSIVE ALLIED RESPONSE TO 'OPERATION SR'

BAD WEATHER FURTHER EAST HAD SO FAR PREVENTED ZEROS FROM REACHING LAE, AS THEY WERE STILL GROUNDED AT GASMATA. THIS MEANT THAT THE EIGHT VF-3 WILDCATS LED BY LT-COMMANDER JIMMY THACH INITIALLY ENCOUNTERED NO AERIAL OPPOSITION OVER LAE, AT LEAST FROM ZEROS.

THERE IS A LOT OF ACTION ABOUT TO HAPPEN BUT FIRST CONSULT THE OPPOSITE MAP TO SEE THE LOCATION OF THE JAPANESE SHIPS WHEN THE ATTACK COMMENCED; THE RED ONES ARE THOSE SUNK IN THE ATTACK.

WHEN THE AMERICANS ARRIVED THE ONLY TWO ENEMY AIRCRAFT TO OPPOSE THEM WERE TWO KIYOKAWA MARU DAVES ALREADY ON PATROL. BOTH MANAGED TO INTERCEPT DEVASTATORS, AN ADVERSARY SLOW ENOUGH FOR THEM TO ATTACK. THREE TBDS RECEIVED BULLET HOLES IN THEIR TAILS . . .

FLYING DAVE R-22 WAS UEMURA HIDEO WITH OBSERVER/ GUNNER AOSHIMA MASABURO. THE DEVASTATOR'S RETURN FIRE DAMAGED ITS FLOATS, AND WHEN EUMURA PUT DOWN, HIS DAVE CAPSIZED AND SANK. THE OTHER DAVE WAS FLOWN BY THE AGGRESSIVE FLYER1c OTOMO TAKUMI, WHO BROKE OFF HIS ATTACK AGAINST THE SLOW DEVASTATORS WHEN FOUR VS-2 DAUNTLESSES INTERVENED.

ADVANCED ENEMY IDENTIFICATION

MOST SECRET

INCREDIBLY, OTOMO SKILFULLY OUTMANOEUVRED ALL THE DAUNTLESS GUNNERS. THE YANKEE BELIGERANTS LATER WROTE THAT THE BIPLANE PILOT HAD FLOWN WITH *"DETERMINATION AND VALOUR"*. TWO WILDCATS NOW ENTERED THE COMBAT. LT 'SCOOP' VORSE NARROWLY MISSED OTOMO JUST BEFORE WINGMAN NOEL GAYLER *"LIFTED HIS NOSE JUST ENOUGH TO SHOOT DOWN THE JAPANESE, THEN KEPT ON WITH HIS OWN STRAFING"*.

OTOMO DROVE HARD INTO HUON GULF WHERE HIS DAVE SHATTERED IN A SHEET OF WHITE SPRAY, COSTING THE LIFE OF BOTH OTOMO & OBSERVER/REAR GUNNER KASAI SHIGEO.

BUT WHAT OF OUR HERO, NEMOTO ?

HE LAUNCHED IN DAVE R-19 ALONGSIDE A SINGLE PETE DURING THE ATTACK. BOTH MANAGED TO ENGAGE RAAF HUDSONS WHICH ARRIVED OVERHEAD FOLLOWING THE USN CARRIER AIRCRAFT. NEMOTO'S OBSERVER/ GUNNER WAS TOSHIJI AONAGI.

A BLACK DAY OFF LAE
10 MARCH 1942

FLYER1C OTOMO TAKUMI CRASHES IN HUON GULF

UEMURA HIDEO DITCHES

WARNED OF THE ATTACK, AT 1000 HOURS NEMOTO CATAPULTED FROM KIYOKAWA MARU TO GUARD IT. HE CLIMBED TO 3,800 METRES AT MAXIMUM POWER WHERE HE PRESSED AN ATTACK AGAINST THREE HUDSONS FROM BEHIND WHICH WERE CRUISING JUST BELOW. ALL THREE WERE HEADED FOR HIS SHIP.

NEMOTO WROTE, *"OWING TO THEIR SUPERIOR SPEED THE GAP BETWEEN US GREW WIDER. THEN OBSERVER TOSHIJI SHOUTED & I TURNED MY HEAD TO SEE THE STARBOARD LANDING WIRE & AERIAL HAD BROKEN AND ONE TAILPLANE BRACE WAS LOOSE AND RATTLING".*

DANGER OF STUCTURAL FAILURE !

ALERT! TAILPLANE BRACE SEVERED !

ALERT! LANDING BRACE BROKEN !

FEARING ENGINE FIRE, NEMOTO FORCE-LANDED JUST OFFSHORE HANISCH BAY. HE MET CURIOUS NATIVES WHO GAVE HIM PAWPAWS & COCONUTS. IN EXCHANGE HE GIFTED THE LOCALS HIS 'THOUSAND STITCHES' COTTON BELLY BAND. A SMALL BOAT FROM DESTROYER MOCHIZUKI APPROACHED TO RESCUE HIM & HIS OBSERVER FROM THE BEACH. NEMOTO SANK R-19, BUT FIRST HE REMOVED ITS GUNS & INSPECTED THE COMBAT DAMAGE. THIS WOULD ENABLE A DETAILED DESCRIPTION FOR HIS SUBSEQUENT LOSS REPORT.

DAMAGED INFLICTED BY RAAF HUDSON A16-163

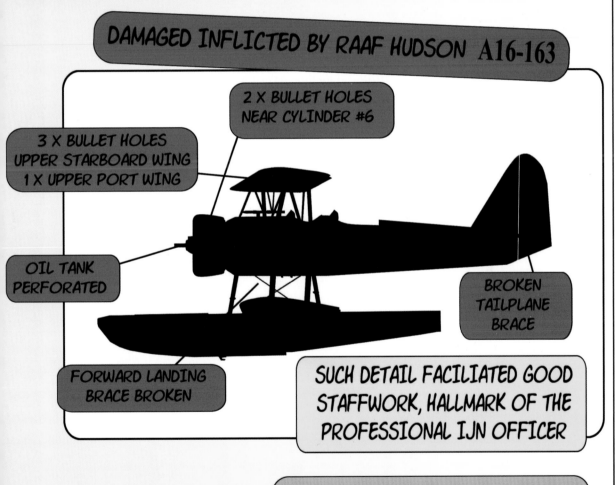

2 X BULLET HOLES NEAR CYLINDER #6

3 X BULLET HOLES UPPER STARBOARD WING 1 X UPPER PORT WING

OIL TANK PERFORATED

BROKEN TAILPLANE BRACE

FORWARD LANDING BRACE BROKEN

SUCH DETAIL FACILIATED GOOD STAFFWORK, HALLMARK OF THE PROFESSIONAL IJN OFFICER

"MORE TERMINOLOGY"

Rear Gunner's Seat Cover
後方銃手席掩蔽
koho jushuseki enpei

THE PLAN HAD ALWAYS BEEN THAT KIYOKAWA MARU'S AIR UNIT WOULD DEPART LAE WHEN ZEROS COULD TAKE OVER. WHEN THE WEATHER CLEARED ON MORNING OF 11 MARCH, THE DAY AFTER THE AMERICAN RAID, REAR-ADMIRAL GOTO ARITOMO AUTHORIZED SEVEN NO. 4 NAVAL AIR GROUP ZEROS ON STANDBY AT GASMATA TO PROCEED TO LAE. THEY ARRIVED THAT MORNING, LED BY LT IWASAKI NOBUHIRO WITH FPO1c YOSHINO SATOSHI, FPO3c KIKUCHI KEIJI, FPO2c SAKAI YOSHIMI, FPO1c NISHIZAWA HIROYOSHI, FPO2c YAMAZAKI ICHIROBEI & FPO2c ITO TSUTOMU.

THE ZEROS WERE INTERSPERSED ACROSS LAE'S REPAIRED DIRT RUNWAY, ABOUT 50 METRES APART, WHILE THEIR PILOTS TOOK IN THE BLEAK SURROUNDS. A DETACHMENT OF G4M1 BETTY BOMBERS SOON FOLLOWED TO CONDUCT SECTOR PATROLS OF THE CORAL SEA, AND TO LATER ATTACK PORT MORESBY.

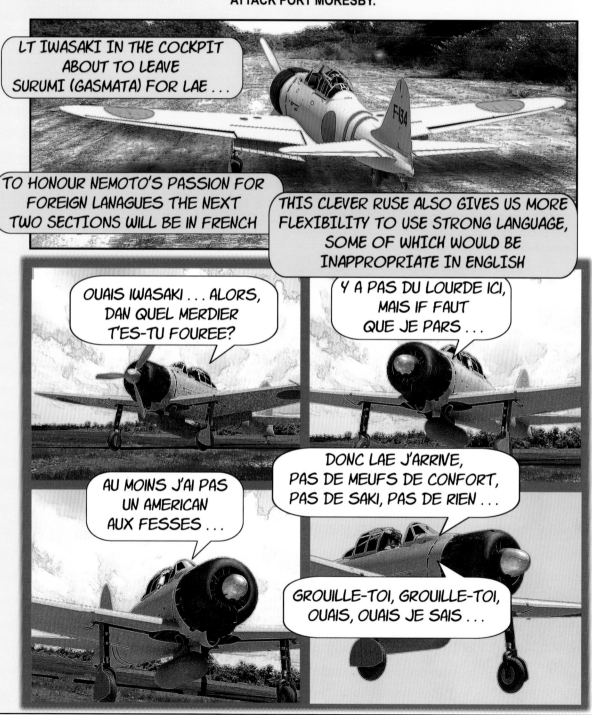

LT IWASAKI IN THE COCKPIT ABOUT TO LEAVE SURUMI (GASMATA) FOR LAE . . .

TO HONOUR NEMOTO'S PASSION FOR FOREIGN LANAGUES THE NEXT TWO SECTIONS WILL BE IN FRENCH

THIS CLEVER RUSE ALSO GIVES US MORE FLEXIBILITY TO USE STRONG LANGUAGE, SOME OF WHICH WOULD BE INAPPROPRIATE IN ENGLISH

OUAIS IWASAKI . . . ALORS, DAN QUEL MERDIER T'ES-TU FOUREE?

Y A PAS DU LOURDE ICI, MAIS IF FAUT QUE JE PARS . . .

AU MOINS J'AI PAS UN AMERICAN AUX FESSES . . .

DONC LAE J'ARRIVE, PAS DE MEUFS DE CONFORT, PAS DE SAKI, PAS DE RIEN . . .

GROUILLE-TOI, GROUILLE-TOI, OUAIS, OUAIS JE SAIS . . .

LE HÉROS ET DÉFENSEUR DE L'EMPIRE ARRIVE À LAE

YOKOHAMA NAVAL AIR GROUP RULES OK. SIMPSON HARBOUR, RABAUL

A RETURN TO THE PEACE AND NORMALITY OF RABAUL

WHEN NEMOTO WAS REUNITED WITH KIYOKAWA MARU HE FOUND IT HAD BEEN BADLY DAMAGED BY ALLIED BOMBS. IT HAD LIMPED BACK TO RABAUL FOR REPAIRS, ARRIVING THERE ON 12 MARCH. BACK ASHORE AT RABAUL NEMOTO HAD TIME TO REFLECT, *"I FEEL STRANGE THAT I AM ALIVE. I CAME THROUGH WITHOUT INJURY. PERHAPS THIS IS THE BEGINNING OF A NEW LIFE."*

RABAUL'S REINVIGORATED CENTRE OF COMMERCE

WHEN HE WALKS AROUND THE TOWN HE FINDS A FEW WELCOME CHANGES. A TEA-HOUSE HAS BEEN OPENED, ALONG WITH A BARBER AND SHOEMAKER, MANAGED BY CHINESE WHO STAYED BEHIND.

HE ESPECIALLY LIKES THE SUGAR SERVED IN THE TEA-HOUSE. IT HAS A DARK BROWN COLOUR SIMILIAR TO THAT SERVED IN JAPAN.

OVER THE NEXT FEW DAYS NEMOTO ENJOYS READING MORE OF TOLSTOI'S 'WAR AND PEACE'. ON 15 MARCH HE RECEIVED A LETTER FROM YOKOSUKA POSTED BY THE WIFE OF JAKE PILOT MATSUE WHO DISAPPEARED WHILE ON A SEARCH ON 20 FEBRUARY. MATSUE'S WIFE POSTED THE LETTER ONLY THREE DAYS BEFORE MATSUE WAS LOST, AND NEMOTO CONFIDES TO HIS DIARY THAT IS *"TERRIBLY SORRY"* FOR THEM BOTH.

MEANWHILE, RABAUL'S MAVIS SEAPLANES CONTINUE LONG-RANGE PATROLS & SOMETIMES BOMB PORT MORESBY.

RABAUL TO PORT MORESBY 430 NAUTICAL MILES, NEARLY THREE HOURS CRUISE

ON 15 MARCH NEMOTO EXPRESSED SEVERAL INCONVENIENT TRUTHS ABOUT THE PERFORMANCE LIMITATIONS OF THE DAVE. HE CONSIDERED THE RESULTS OF HIS COMBAT WITH THE USN WERE, *"A GREAT ACHIEVEMENT, GIVEN THE LIMITATIONS OF THE TYPE I FLEW THAT DAY. WHY ? BECAUSE THE TYPE 95 HAS THE EFFICIENCY OF A TRAINER. WE NEED MORE SUPERIOR FLOATPLANES. THE TYPE 95 WILL NOT DO. I HOPE JAPANESE TECHNOLOGY WILL IMPROVE."*

NEMOTO HAD A VALID POINT. THE DAVE WAS ALREADY OBSOLETE. SEE BELOW TO BETTER UNDERSTAND ITS PERFORMANCE LIMITATIONS.

TWIN 7.7 MM MACHINE GUNS

CANVASS-COVERED AIRFRAME

CRUISE 100 KTS MAX SPEED 160 KTS

FIXED PITCH PROPELLER

KOTOBUKI 630HP RADIAL ENGINE

IRONY LIES IN THE FACT THAT THE DAVE'S 9-CYLINDER KOTOBUKI RADIAL HAD BEEN DEVELOPED UNDER LICENCE FROM THE BRITISH BRISTOL JUPITER ENGINE.

Longevity

寿

kotobuki

MEANWHILE RABAUL'S NEARBY VOLCANO HAD BEEN PLAYING UP. NEMOTO COMPLAINS THAT WHITE ASH IS COVERING MOST OF THE TOWN WHICH HE FINDS *"RATHER UNPLEASANT"*. ON 20 MARCH HE FINDS OUT THAT HIS SHIP WILL RETURN TO JAPAN TO REPAIR THE DAMAGE INFLICTED BY THE USN ATTACK NEAR LAE. THE GOOD NEWS IS HE IS TO BE ENDORSED TO FLY THE PETE, AND ALSO THAT HE MIGHT BE PROMOTED IN OCTOBER.

HE ALSO HOPES HIS MOTHER IS IN GOOD HEALTH IN JAPAN, BUT COMPLAINS THAT HIS CABIN HAS TOO MANY COCKROACHES. FOR THE NEXT WEEK OR SO HE CONTINUES PATROLS AROUND RABAUL

A VOLCANO ON WEST NEW BRITAIN

NEW BRITAIN'S IMPENETRABLE JUNGLE. MANY UNDISCOVERED WW2 AIRCRAFT WRECKS STILL LIE HERE

THUS KIYOKAWA MARU LEAVES RABAUL ON 27 MARCH. JUST BEFORE SAILING, AN AIRCRAFT ENGINEER IS HIT BY A SPINNING PROPELLER WHILE WORKING ON DECK. HE LATER DIES AT RABAUL NAVY HOSPITAL.

NEMOTO REALISES THE FOLLOWING DAY HE HAS LEFT HIS SPARE SUMMER & SPRING UNIFORMS IN DRAWERS UNDER HIS CABIN BED ON KIYOKAWA MARU. NOW THAT THE SHIP HAS SAILED HE REPROACHES HIS FORGETFULNESS.

ON 30 MARCH NEMOTO TAKES A JAKE ON A SIX-HOUR PATROL. HE NOTES THAT THE MOON WAS BEAUTIFUL AND WHEN HE RETURNED TO MALAGUNA HE ENJOYED A BEER WHILE WATCHING ITS CIRCLE IN THE NIGHT SKY, AND THAT *"THE WIND WAS COOL AND PLEASANT"*.

BOTH THE ZEROS AND BETTY ARE FROM NO. 4 NAVAL AIR GROUP

MEANWHILE THE AIR WAR IS HOTTING UP AT RABAUL. NO 4 NAVAL AIR GROUP HAS STARTED BOMBING PORT MORESBY FROM RABAUL AND LAE, ESCORTED BY LAE-BASED ZEROS FROM THE SAME NAVAL AIR GROUP.

THIS FORTRESS STILL CARRIES STRIPED RUDDER MARKINGS

NEMOTO NOTES THAT RABAUL IS SOMETIMES RAIDED BY FLYING FORTRESSES BUT IS DISAPPOINTED THAT NONE HAVE BEEN SHOT DOWN.

ON EVENING OF 5 APRIL NEMOTO & COMRADES WATCHED SEVERAL MOVIES, VIA A PROJECTOR LENT TO THEM FROM ANOTHER SHIP. THE MAIN FEATURE WAS AN ANIMÉ FILM MADE BY JAPANESE COMEDIAN FURUKAWA ROPPA, A POPULAR COMEDIAN

THE FILM WAS 男の花道, WHICH TRANSLATES AS 'MAN'S PATH OF FLOWERS'.

FURUKAWA ROPPA
1903-61

ON 9 APRIL NEMOTO RECEIVED THE GOOD NEWS THAT KIYOKAWA MARU HAD REACHED YOKOSUKA SAFELY THE PREVIOUS AFTERNOON. HE FREQUENTLY REFERS TO AIR-RAIDS INCLUDING ONE AGAINST SALAMAUA WHERE HE WAS TOLD THAT THE BELIGERENTS WERE VICKERS WELLINGTON BOMBERS (IN FACT B-26 MARAUDERS). ON 17 APRIL HE FLEW A LONG PATROL OF FIVE HOURS, DURING WHICH NEMOTO DROPPED HIS CAP OVERBOARD. HE HOPES HIS SHIP WILL SOON RETURN SO HE CAN RETURN TO THE FRONT LINES.

RENDERED UNSERVICEABLE BY AUSTRALIAN SOLDIERS

ON 22 APRIL NEMOTO AND FIVE OTHERS HAD LEAVE SO THEY TOOK A TRIP DOWN TO THE COASTAL TOWN OF KOKOPO BY CAR, PASSING WHERE THEIR TROOPS HAD INVADED ON 23 JANUARY. THEY WENT TO THE MILITARY POLICE POST AT KOKOPO TO BUY SAKE & BEER, HOWEVER NONE WAS IN STOCK. THEY FOUND AN ABANDONNED TRUCK BUT THE CARBURETTOR & OTHER KEY PARTS HAD BEEN REMOVED BY THE AUSTRALIANS PRIOR TO INVASION

AROUND LUNCH THEY WERE DRIVEN AROUND BY A "BRITISH PRISONER" (ACTUALLY AUSTRALIAN) FOR ABOUT 40 MINUTES. ALL THE NATIVES BOWED AS THEY PASSED, OF WHICH NEMOTO WROTE, "I UNDERSTAND THE LOCALS HAVE BEEN DISCIPLINED SINCE THE OCCUPATION". NEMOTO TOOK TEA WITH A FAMILY HE JUDGED TO BE MALAYAN, HOWEVER HE FOUND COMMUNICATING WITH THEM DIFFICULT DUE TO HIS POOR ENGLISH. HOWEVER, HE REALLY ENJOYED THE TRIP.

THEN, WITH LITTLE WARNING ALL PILOTS WERE PARADED AT 1200 AT MALAGUNA WHERE INFORMED THAT THEY WOULD BECOME PART OF THE TULAGI INVASION IN THE SOLOMONS.

NEMOTO IS ORDERED TO LEAD TWO DAVES TO THE SHORTLAND ISLANDS, THEN AWAIT FURTHER INSTRUCTIONS.

NEMOTO FLIES FROM RABAUL TO THE SHORTLAND ISLANDS, AT THE SOUTHERN TIP OF BOUGAINVILLE WHERE THERE IS A SEAPLANE BASE. THE 280 NAUTICAL-MILE-FLIGHT TAKES JUST SHORT OF THREE HOURS. THE TWO CREWS ARE QUARTERED IN A COMFY PLANTATION HOUSE, ABOUT 20 MINUTES WALK FROM THE BEACH.

THE HOUSE HAD BEEN ABANDONNED AT SHORT NOTICE. NEMOTO WRITES, "*I CAN TELL FROM THE DOUBLE BED AND KITCHEN THAT PEOPLE RECENTLY LIVED HERE. THERE ARE A NUMBER OF BOOKS, IN ENGLISH, ON THE SHELF. I WALKED INTO THE NEARBY TREES AND FOUND A DOZEN WANDERING COWS. THERE ARE ALSO MANY WILD LEMON TREES.*"

COULD THERE BE A BASIS HERE FOR AN ANIMÉ FEATURE TITLED 'NEMO ROSSO' ?

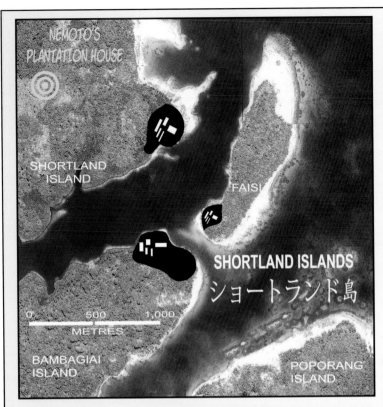

NEMOTO'S PLANTATION HOUSE

SHORTLAND ISLAND

FAISI

SHORTLAND ISLANDS
ショートランド島

0   500   1,000
METRES

BAMBAGIAI ISLAND

POPORANG ISLAND

NEMOTO & ACCOMPLICES SPEND FIVE NIGHTS AT THE ISLAND BASE. ON 2 MAY 'COMFORT BAGS' ARRIVED FROM JAPAN, DELIVERED BY MAVIS FLYING BOAT FROM RABAUL.

HOWEVER, THIS IS TRULY THE CALM BEFORE THE STORM. IN THE VERY EARLY DARK MORNING OF 3 MAY AT 0130 THE PILOTS ASSEMBLE AND ARE BRIEFED ON 'Z' DAY - THE INVASION OF TULAGI. THEY LAUNCH SHORTLY THEREAFTER FOR TULAGI, OFFSHORE GUADALCANAL, A NAME WHICH WILL SOON FEATURE ON THE FRONT PAGE OF EVERY US NEWSPAPER.

BOUGAINVILLE

IJN LAUNCH RUNS SHUTTLE BETWEEN THE THREE ISLANDS + BOUGAINVILLE

SLEEPY SHORTLAND ISLAND

THE BONZA RAAF BASE AT GAVUTU

GUADALCANAL 18 NM

RABAUL 550 NM

THE ISLAND BASE OFFSHORE TULAGI CALLED GAVUTU WAS HOME TO RAAF CATALINAS. FROM LATE JANUARY 1942 ONWARDS MAVIS FLYING BOATS STARTED BOMBING THE SMALL AUSTRALIAN GARRISON THERE WHICH HAD ONLY WW1 VICKERS MACHINE GUNS FOR DEFENCE. THESE RAIDS DID LITTLE DAMAGE HOWEVER & THE AUSTRALIANS ENTERTAINED THEMSELVES BY BUILDING DUMMY TARGETS AS DECOYS. THEN ON 18 MARCH, NO. 1 NAVAL AIR GROUP NELL BOMBERS, COMMANDED BY LIEUTENANT KANEKO YOSHIO, ACTUALLY HELPED THE AUSSIES DEMOLISH THE ISLAND'S INFRASTRUCTURE PRIOR TO THE ANTICIPATED JAPANESE OCCUPATION!

HEY MATE CHUCK US A LINE WILL YA? IS THE BARBY + PISS-UP STILL ON TONIGHT?

HEY BLUE, D'JA SEE ANY BEAUT SHEILAS IN SNAKE GULLEY?

GAVUTU WAS NOT AS COMFORTABLE AS RABAUL ALTHOUGH IT HAD A NICE CLUB AT NEARBY TULAGI. THE AUSSIES AT THE RAAF BASE SPOKE A UNIQUE SLANG WHICH IS A WONDER TO BEHOLD. ITS INHERENT VOCABULARY IS AN ONGOING EXPRESSIONIST GIFT TO THE ENGLISH-SPEAKING WORLD.

"ANOTHER USEFUL TECHNICAL TERM!"

Bomb release gear
爆彈投下始動裝置
toka shido sochi

WW1 VICKERS MACHINE-GUN

THE CATALINAS USUALLY DEPARTED GAVUTU EARLY MORNING & RETURNED LATE IN THE DAY, THUS AVOIDING AIR-RAIDS. THEIR JOB WAS MAINLY PROVIDING RECONNAISSANCE OF THE SOLOMONS AND BOUGAINVILLE.

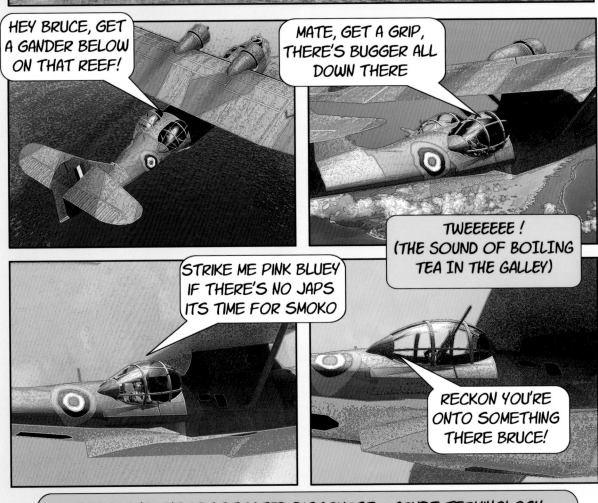

THE ABOVE UNSOPHISTICATED DISCOURSE + CRUDE TERMINOLOGY UNDERLINE THAT THESE PATROLS RARELY FOUND ANYTHING WORTHWHILE.

ON 30 APRIL THREE MAVIS DEPARTED RABAUL VERY EARLY AT 0350, LED BY YOKOHAMA NAVAL AIR GROUP OPERATIONS OFFICER COMMANDER TASHIRO SOICHI. THE TRIO ARRIVED OVERHEAD TULAGI AT 0655 WHERE THEY FOUND TWO CATALINAS MOORED BELOW. AFTER DROPPING 250 & 60 KG BOMBS, TASHIRO'S MASSIVE FLYING BOATS THEN DESCENDED AND STRAFED THE RAAF BASE WITH 20MM CANNON FIRE. SUCH LOW-LEVEL TACTICS WERE RARE FOR MAVIS.

PILOT BILL MILLER FLEW THE LAST RAAF CAT OUT OF TULAGI, DEPARTING WITH ANOTHER CAT BEFORE DAWN ON 2 MAY. THUS ENDED THE RAAF WARTIME ERA AT THE BASE.

WHILE FLYING TOWARDS PORT MORESBY, MILLER'S WIRELESS OPERATOR OVERHEARD TRANSMISSIONS DURING A RAID AGAINST TULAGI BY TWO MAVIS FLYING BOATS.

THIS ZERO MISSION BY SHOHO WAS REVEALED FOR THE FIRST TIME IN VOL 3 OF SOUTH PACIFIC AIR WAR BY AVONMORE BOOKS.

AND SO THESE BRITISH SCOUNDRELS + RUFFIANS WILL BE TAUGHT ANOTHER LESSON

DANG, WE'RE A LONG WAY FROM THE SHIP . . .

AND SO THE 'SHOHO THREE' DESCEND TOWARDS TULAGI TO ROUGH UP THE PLACE A TAD

BLAM!

THE TWO MAVIS WERE LED BY THEIR OLD FRIEND TOSHIRO, AND SHORTLY THEREAFTER THREE ZEROS FROM SHOHO STRAFED TULAGI IN A MISSION CLASSIFIED AS "INTIMIDATION". THE ZEROS WERE FOLLOWED BY FLOATPLANE ATTACKS, COURTESY OF KAMIKAWA MARU (NOT KIYOKAWA MARU) JAKES BASED BRIEFLY AT REKATA BAY.

IN REALITY NEMOTO WAS A BUT SMALL COG IN 'OPERATION MO' THE OPERATION TO CAPTURE TULAGI & PORT MORESY. THE STRATEGY WAS FOR YOKOHAMA NAVAL AIR GROUP MAVIS FLYING BOATS TO SET UP BASE AT TULAGI, WHILE NELL BOMBERS WOULD FLY LONG-RANGE MISSIONS FROM VUNAKANAU, RABAUL.

RAAF CATALINA BASE
GAVUTU, BRITISH SOLOMON ISLANDS

Tanambogo

Gavutu

NEMOTO'S TWO DAVES ARRIVE AT GAVUTU ON AFTERNOON OF 3 MAY, JUST AFTER ITS CAPTURE

METRES
0   100   200   300

WHEN PORT MORESBY WAS CAPTURED, NO. 4 NAVAL AIR GROUP BETTYS & ZEROS FROM THE TAINAN NAVAL AIR GROUP WOULD SET UP BASE THERE . . .

AT LEAST, THAT WAS THE PLAN.

ROAAAR

THE JAPANESE HAD NO IDEA THAT A USN CARRIER FORCE WAS LURKING NEARBY . . .

A SURPRISE WAS TRULY IN THE OFFING . . .

AGAIN

81

4 MAY 1942, 0630 HOURS LAUNCHING FROM YORKTOWN IN BLUSTERY 35-KNOT WIND HEADED FOR TULAGI

INCLEMENT + CAPRICIOUS WEATHER PRESAGED THE LAUNCH. THIS WAS CHALLENGING

T'WERE LOW CLOUD COVER & STRONG WINDS WHICH WITNESSED FORTY DEVASTATORS & SBDs LAUNCH FROM USN CARRIER YORKTOWN ABOUT A HUNDRED MILES SOUTH OF TULAGI. AND, THIS WAS ONLY THE FIRST STRIKE OF THE DAY . . .

"THESE UNLETTERED MISCREANTS HAVE HAD IT COMING"

"WONDER IF THERE WILL BE ANY AERIAL OPPOSITION WITH RED CIRCLES"

THESE TOUGH USN DIVE-BOMBER PILOTS CERTAINLY HAD WICKED INTENTIONS

WAY TO GO . . . BOMBS 4 NIPPON, TRYING TIMES FOR TOJO

SO, THESE ARE 28 SBDS FROM YORKTOWN'S VS-5 + VB-5

THESE DUDES ARE ABOUT TO RUIN NEMOTO'S DAY, AND THAT OF HIS CHUMS TOO !

SET TO LADS . . .
LOOKS LIKE THERE IS
NO-ONE HERE TO OPPOSE
OUR GALLANT QUEST

JUST AFTER 0800 THE SBDS APPROACHED TULAGI WHERE THE PILOTS SAW SHIPPING AT ANCHOR. OVER THE HARBOUR AREA THE SBDs PEELED OFF TO MAKE DIVE-BOMBING RUNS FROM 10,000 FEET, TARGETING MINE-LAYER OKINOSHIMA & TWO DESTROYERS.

SETTING SITES ON OKINOSHIMA

NEXT TO ATTACK WERE TBDS AT LOW LEVEL. THE SHIPS' AA DEFENCES FIRED TO RETALIATE, INCLUDING OKINOSHIMA'S FOUR 5-INCH HIGH-ANGLE GUNS. THE AMERICAN AIRCREWS LATER REPORTED THIS RETURN FIRE AS *"HEAVY BUT INEFFECTIVE"*.

BLAM!

A FLEEING FELLOW!

JUST MISSED THE PALM TREE

ENOUGH OF THE YANKEES ! LET'S GO DOWN BELOW TO SEE WHAT'S HAPPENING TO NEMOTO & COMRADES, CLEARLY ON THE WRONG END OF THE STICK . . .

THE COMFY FORMER RAAF BARRACKS OCCUPIED BY NEMOTO ET AL ON GAVUTU

OF THE DAY'S TUMULTUOUS EVENTS, NEMOTO WROTE, *"AT 0610 WERE WERE RESTING IN THE GAVUTU BARRACKS WHEN APPROXIMATELY FIFTEEN ENEMY PLANES CLOSED IN AT 3,500 METRES FROM THE EAST. OUR PATROLS WERE NOT DUE TO COMMENCE UNTIL 0700 SO WE HAD NO FLOATPLANES AIRBORNE. OBSERVATION PLANE R-13 WAS ABOUT TO TAKE OFF WHEN IT WAS MACHINE-GUNNED . . . "*

THE PETE WAS STRAFED BY A SOLE SBD WHICH HAD JUST FINISHED ITS DIVE-BOMBING RUN. R-13 BURST INTO FLAMES AFTER ITS FUEL TANK WAS HIT. A RESCUE LAUNCH RETRIEVED BADLY-BURNED PILOT FLYER1c NUNOKAWA, ALSO WOUNDED IN THE CHEST. HE WAS TAKEN ASHORE BUT DIED EARLY THAT AFTERNOON. NEMOTO HAD JUST LOST ANOTHER COMRADE.

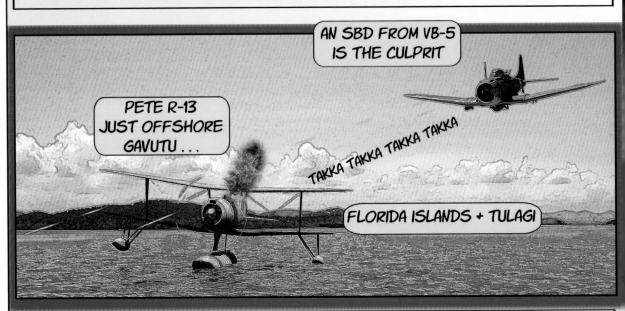

AN SBD FROM VB-5 IS THE CULPRIT

PETE R-13 JUST OFFSHORE GAVUTU . . .

TAKKA TAKKA TAKKA TAKKA

FLORIDA ISLANDS + TULAGI

BY ABOUT 0930 ALL THE USN ATTACKERS HAD SAFELY RETURNED TO YORKTOWN. FOLLOWING AN URGENT DEBRIEF, ADMIRAL FRANK FLETCHER DECIDED TO LAUNCH ANOTHER STRIKE. CARRIER CREWS REFUELLED & REARMED 38 AIRCRAFT TO RETURN TO TULAGI/ GAVUTU.

SINCE THE FIRST RAID HAD MET NO AERIAL OPPOSITION, THE WILDCATS WOULD REMAIN OVERHEAD THE CARRIER TO DEFEND IT.

WHILE ALL THIS WAS GOING ON, NEMOTO RACED TO TULAGI ABOARD AN IJN LAUNCH SEEKING MEDICAL HELP FOR THE INJURED NUNOKAWA

GUARDING 'YORKTOWN'

BACK INTO THE RING FOR ANOTHER SWING . . .

BUT THIS TIME THE ATTACKERS WOULD FIND MORE THAN JUST SHIPS IN THEIR SITES . . .

THIS SBD IS FROM VS-5

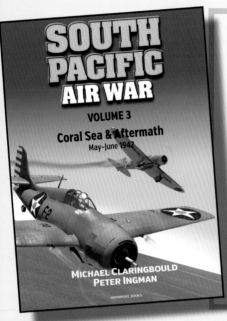

SOUTH PACIFIC AIR WAR

VOLUME 3

Coral Sea & Aftermath
May-June 1942

MICHAEL CLARINGBOULD
Peter Ingman

AVONMORE BOOKS

NOT SURPRISINGLY, NEMOTO MAKES NO MENTION DURING THIS FRACAS OF WHO MIGHT RESPONSIBLY RECORD THIS PIECE OF INTRIGUING HISTORY IN THE FUTURE. HOWEVER, HIS MIND WOULD HAVE BEEN SET AT EASE HAD HE KNOWN THAT VOL 3 OF 'SOUTH PACIFIC AIR WAR' WOULD COVER THE ATTACK IN DETAIL, DELVING INTO THE MINUITAE OF BOTH SIDES, ASSEMBLING THEM LIKE A JIGSAW, AND RESOLVING MANY MYTHS OF THE ERA.

PUBLISHED BY AVONMOREBOOKS AUSTRALIA, THIS GROUND-BREAKING SERIES IS THE FIRST TO CONSISTENTLY & CAREFULLY RECONCILE OFFICIAL RECORDS FROM BOTH SIDES. HAVE WE RAISED THIS PREVIOUSLY?

IT IS ALSO THE FIRST HISTORICAL SERIES TO ACCURATELY DEPICT & DEFINE THE MARKINGS OF BOTH ALLIED & JAPANESE BELLIGERENTS

BUT NOW WE RETURN TO THE EXCITEMENT OF THE SECOND USN ATTACK. SHORTLY AFTER IT COMMENCED AN AMERICAN PILOT SHOUTED *"JAP SEAPLANE!"* OVER THE RADIO. THIS WAS ONE OF THREE FLOATPLANES, A DAVE AND TWO PETES, WHICH HAD LAUNCHED IMMEDIATELY AFTER THE FIRST ATTACK HAD FINISHED.

A DANG BIPLANE! WHAT KIND OF (EXPLETIVE DELETED) STRING BAG IS THIS?

BLAM!

KUMAZAWA'S R-12 IN THE DRINK

R-12 WAS DISPATCHED BY A VS-5 DAUNTLESS, BUT PILOT FPO3c MATSUZAWA & OBSERVER FPO1c KUMAZAWA TAKASHI WERE RESCUED BACK TO GAVUTU. KIYOKAWA MARU BUNTAICHO LT TAKEDA HIDEO PILOTED THE SECOND PETE, BUT ALMOST RAN OUT OF FUEL. HE TAXIED ONTO THE BEACH & CLAMBERED INTO PETE R-14. IT WOULD NOT START, SO HE GRABBED DAVE R-23 & DUELED WITH MORE SBDs, RETURNING TO GAVUTU WITH R-23 MUCH WORSE FOR WEAR.

THE E8N2 DAVE FLOWN BY BUNTAICHO LT TAKEDA HIDEO ON 4 MAY; HIS SUDDEN PLAN 'B' WHEN HE COULD NOT START THE ENGINE OF A NEARBY FULLY-REFUELLED PETE. HE RETURNED R-23 WITH SEVERAL BULLET HOLES, COURTESY OF SBD GUNS.

NOW WE RETURN DIRECTLY TO OUR HERO NEMOTO . . . WHEN HE RETURNED TO GAVUTU FROM TULAGI BY LAUNCH, HE SAW A PETE APPROACH FROM THE WEST, ACTUALLY FROM KAMIKAWA MARU, BEING ONE OF SIX FROM THAT SHIP ORDERED TO SUPPORT THE TULAGI OPERATION.

NEMOTO WAS UNAWARE THAT TWO OF ITS COMRADES HAD JUST BEEN SHOT DOWN BY THE WILDCATS. A RADIO CALL TOLD GAVUTU THAT AN ENEMY AIRCRAFT CRASHED TEN MILES FROM TULAGI, BUT IN FACT THIS WAS THE PETE NEMOTO HAD SEEN IN THE DISTANCE, & THE FINAL ONE SHOT DOWN BY WILDCATS. NEMOTO TOOK OFF IN HIS DAVE & SEARCHED UNSUCCESSFULLY FOR IT, *"THE SUN WAS ABOUT TO SET SO I TURNED BACK . . . IT IS HOPELESS WHEN ONE AIRCRAFT IS AGAINST SIX. TULAGI BASE IS A BIG BLACK SPOT."*

END OF A PETE FROM KAMIKAWA MARU

BLAM!

BLAM!

ZI-12

KAMIKAWA MARU TAIL PREFIX 'ZI'

FINAL ADVENTURES AT TULAGI ON 4 MAY

THE FIRST SHOTAI ARRIVES LATE AT TULAGI/ GAVUTU

THESE KAMIKAWA MARU PETES TO WHICH NEMOTO REFERRED WERE THE SECOND FLIGHT OF THREE OF A TOTAL OF SIX TEMPORARILY BASED IN THE SHORTLANDS. ALL HAD DEPARTED THE ISLAND BASE AT 1115 TO REINFORCE TULAGI. THE FIRST FLIGHT HAD BEEN DISTRACTED BY ATTACKING A RAAF CATALINA, LUCKILY DELAYING THEIR ARRIVAL AT GAVUTU UNTIL AFTER THE USN RAID HAD FINISHED.

MEANHILE THE VF-42 WILDCATS WHICH SHOT DOWN THE ENTIRE SECOND FLIGHT OF PETES WERE IMPRESSED WITH THE FIGHTER-LIKE QUALITIES OF THEIR ADVERSARIES.

6 MAY 1942 HEADING FOR DEBOYNE JUST BEFORE LUNCH

DID YOU BRING A MAGAZINE TO READ SEAMAN?

YE OLDE FAITHFUL KOTOBUKI . . . HUUUUMMMM

ARE WE THERE YET?

THE 'LONGEVITY' POWER-PLANT, 'OLE RELIABLE'

AS PREVIOUSLY STATED, NEMOTO WAS A BUT SMALL COG IN 'OPERATION MO' THE IJN OPERATION TO CAPTURE TULAGI & PORT MORESBY. WITH TULAGI NOW SECURED, NEMOTO WAS RESTATIONED TO AN 'ADVANCE GROUP', WHERE A TEMPORARY SEAPLANE BASE WOULD GUARD VITAL PROTECTIVE WAYPOINTS OF THE APPROACHING CONVOY. NEMOTO'S NEW POST WAS DEBOYNE ISLAND IN THE LOUISIADE ARCHIPELIGO.

THE DAVE'S RANGE WAS INSUFFICIENT TO FLY THERE DIRECTLY, SO ON 5 MAY HE RETURNED TO THE SHORTLANDS BASE WHERE HE OVER-NIGHTED. HE DEPARTED NEXT DAY FOR A THREE-HOUR FLIGHT TO DEBOYNE ISLAND.

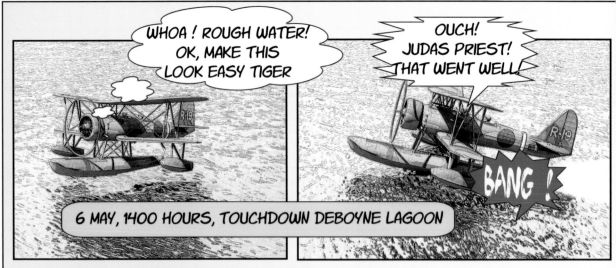

6 MAY, 1400 HOURS, TOUCHDOWN DEBOYNE LAGOON

OH NOOOO - THIS IS AWKWARD ! WHEN HE ARRIVES, NEMOTO LANDS BADLY IN ROUGH WATER, AND DAMAGES A FLOAT. ON 7 MAY HIS DAVE IS HOISTED ABOARD KAMIKAWA MARU, ALREADY AT THE LAGOON. THE PLAN IS TO REPAIR HIS FLOATPLANE ABOARD THE SHIP. MEANWHILE THE INVASION OF PORT MORESBY PROCEEDS . . .

Fuselage truss wire
胴體航空用張金
dotai kokuyo harigane

WE ARE NOT PRIVY AS TO WHETHER NEMOTO HARBOURED A POST-WAR CAREER AS A FILM MAKER, HOWEVER IF SO, THE ARRIVAL AT DEBOYNE WOULD SURELY HAVE FEATURED.

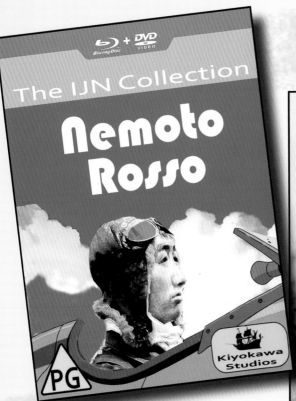

The IJN Collection

Nemoto Rosso

Kiyokawa Studios

PG

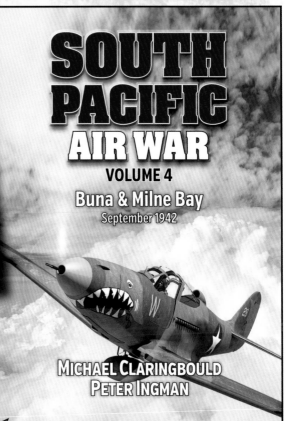

SOUTH PACIFIC

AIR WAR

VOLUME 4

Buna & Milne Bay
September 1942

MICHAEL CLARINGBOULD
PETER INGMAN

ALAS, HE FEATURES BUT LIGHTLY IN VOLUME 4 OF SOUTH PACIFIC AIR WAR, FOR GLARING REASONS WHICH WILL SOON MATERIALIZE.

MASSIVE BATTLE OCCURING OVER THE HORIZON

THINGS WERE BUZZING AT DEBOYNE LAGOON, WHERE ALONGSIDE DAVES, JAKES & PETES FROM THE TWO SEAPLANE TENDERS, THERE WERE ALSO OBSOLETE E7K ALFS FLOATPLANES OF THE 6TH CRUISER SENTAI.

NEMOTO SPENT MOST OF 7 MAY UNLOADING SUPPLIES ONTO THE BEACH AT HIS NEW ISLAND BASE, WHERE THE THE SCENERY WAS STUNNING.

WHAT NONE AT THE DEBOYNE BASE REALISED WAS THAT NOT FAR AWAY ONE OF THE PACIFIC WAR'S DETERMINING BATTLES WAS UNFOLDING:

BATTLE OF THE CORAL SEA

GIV-1

E7K ALF OBSERVATION FLOAT-PLANE WITH CREW OF THREE FROM CRUISER FURUTAKA

THIS MAMMOTH CLASH HAD HUNDREDS OF WORKING PARTS, HOWEVER WE SHALL SEE IT THROUGH NEMOTO'S EYES. ON 7 MAY HE WROTE, *"TODAY WE RECIEVED A REPORT THAT AN ENEMY FORMATION WAS APPROACHING. . ."* THE JAPANESE AT DEBOYNE HAD THE DETAILS WRONG, HOWEVER THEY WELL UNDERSTOOD THE GRAVITY OF THE SITUATION.

MEANWHILE NOT FAR AWAY OVER MISIMA . . .

"AIM TRUE MY BOY. GOLLY, THIS FELLOW HAS TROUBLE APPROACHING"

MENACE IN DE GUISE

A VF-2 WILDCAT DOES ITS WORK ON 7 MAY

BLAM!

ENEMY IDENTIFICATION

THE ABOVE INCIDENT OCCURRED WHEN PATROLLING VF-2 WILDCATS APPROACHING MISIMA ISLAND SPOTTED A BIPLANE HEADED THEIR WAY AT 12 O'CLOCK LOW. THEIR GUNFIRE FORCED IT TO DITCH, HOWEVER THE CREW WAS RESCUED BY AN IJN LAUNCH, BUT NOT BEFORE THEY SANK THEIR OWN FURUTAKA-BASED ALF SO IT COULD NOT BE CAPTURED.

SECRET

THEIRS   THEIRS   OURS   OURS

WHEN SHOHO WAS SUNK, ONE OF ITS CLAUDES & TWO ZEROS WERE STILL ALOFT. WITH THEIR CARRIER SUNK, THEY HEADED TO DEBOYNE, 30 MILES SOUTH-WEST. THESE WERE CLAUDE PILOT FPO3c ISHIKAWA SHIRO, AND ZERO PILOTS BUNTAICHO LT NOTOMI KENJIRO & FPO2c TAMURA SHUNICHI. ALL THREE DITCHED IN THE PICTURESQUE LAGOON, ADJACENT TO AN ANCHORED MERCHANTMAN, AS WITNESSED BY NEMOTO, "*ONE AFTER ANOTHER, THEY CAPSIZED IN THE WATER WITH A DREADFUL SPLASH*". THE PILOTS LATER RETURNED TO RABAUL ABOARD KAMIKAWA MARU.

MEANWHILE, NO. 4 NAVAL AIR GROUP BETTY BOMBER TAIL F-378 COMMANDED BY FPO1c SUGII MISAO WAS IN BIG TROUBLE. AN EXPERIENCED COMBAT PILOT, HIS BOMBER HAD BEEN HIT BY THICK AA FIRE KNOCKING OUT THE LEFT ENGINE. THE SAME BLAST HAD KILLED THE RADIO OPERATOR & BADLY WOUNDED THE COPILOT.

THINGS WERE NOT GOING WELL . . .

NOW THAT THE CREW HA̶V̶E̶ ⤬HAS HAS BEEN RESCUED, WE CAN RETURN TO THE NARRATIVE . . .

LATER THAT DAY SOME OF THE CREW RETURN WITH A SMALL PLANTATION BOAT TO RETRIEVE ORDNANCE & OTHER USEFUL EQUIPMENT.

ON 8 MAY THE BATTLE CONTINUED TO RAGE OUT AT SEA, & NEWS SOON SPREAD AROUND DEBOYNE THAT THE IJN HAD SUNK CARRIER USS SARATOGA. THIS WAS MISTAKEN IDENTITY HOWEVER, AS YORKTOWN & LEXINGTON WERE THE ONLY TWO USN CARRIERS IN THE BATTLE.

NEMOTO WROTE, "AT 1500 A FIGHTER FROM ZUIKAKU MADE A FORCED-LANDING. HE TOLD US A VIVID STORY OF TODAY'S BATTLE. TWO ENEMY CARRIERS WERE SUNK BY OUR TORPEDOS AND HE SHOT DOWN THREE ENEMIES."

ZUIKAKU ZERO PILOT FPO2C OKURA SHIGERU

LOW ON FUEL! WHERE THE *+%$ HELL IS MY CARRIER?

NO SAKE 4 ME 2NITE! LOOKS LIKE I WILL SPEND THE EVENING ON SOME FLEA-BITTEN ISLAND

THAT'S DEBOYNE AHEAD WELL HERE GOES, SHIGERU-SAN MY BOY! OPEN THE CANOPY!

JUST WAIT TILL I TELL THE CHAPS DOWN THERE I BLASTED THREE YANKEES OUTA THE SKY!

SPLASH TIME. ELECTRICS OFF KILL MIXTURE TANK JETTISONED - CHECK

EVER GET THE FEELING THE ILLUSTRATOR IS ELONGATING THIS SEQUENCE TO SHOWCASE HIS SKILL AT OCEAN ART?

NO NEED TO WORRY ABOUT ZUIKAKU PILOT FPO2C OKURA SHIGERU

C'EST LE COOL T'AS FAIT BON MON MEC BRAVE

WITHIN MINUTES HE IS ABOARD A RESCUE LAUNCH, AND SOON TALKING TO NEMOTO

THAT SAME MORNING THE DEBOYNE BASE WAS IDENTIFIED BY THE ALLIES, WITH NINE FLOATPLANES SEEN MOORED ALONG THE BEACH. A B-25 MITCHELL STRAFED THE BASE THAT ARVO. NEMOTO, WHO HAD NEVER SEEN A MITCHELL BEFORE, THOUGHT IT WAS A 'LOCKHEED' [HUDSON], AND TOLD HIS DIARY THAT THE BOMBER STRAFED THE BASE WITH NO CASUALTIES, BUT DAMAGED SEVERAL FLOATPLANES.

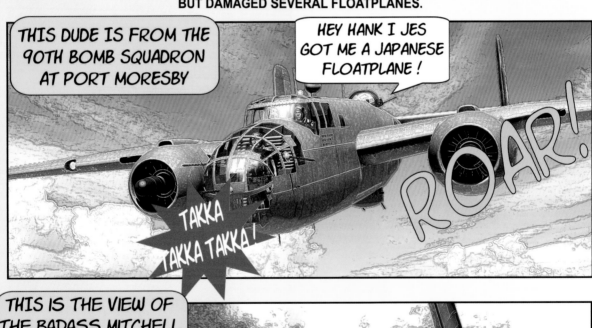

THIS DUDE IS FROM THE 90TH BOMB SQUADRON AT PORT MORESBY

HEY HANK I JES GOT ME A JAPANESE FLOATPLANE !

TAKKA TAKKA TAKKA!

ROAR!

THIS IS THE VIEW OF THE BADASS MITCHELL FROM THE BEACH

THE USAAF INVADER EVEN USED HIS LOWER TURRET GUN TO STIR UP TROUBLE!

BLAMMO!

THERE WAS NOT ENOUGH TIME TO REMOVE THE INSTRUMENT PANEL FROM OKURA'S ZERO

MANY NERVOUS INCUMBENTS ON DEBOYNE . . .

"YOU CAN COME OUT FROM BEHIND THAT TREE PETTY OFFICER, ITS ONE OF OURS"

IN THESE FEW DAYS WINNERS + LOSERS ALL OVER THE PACIFIC

KEEPING WATCH FROM DEBOYNE . . .

"AN EMPIRE IMPERIALIST ! "

KEEPING WATCH FROM DEBOYNE . . .

"NOT GOOD PETTY OFFICER, THAT'S A BRITISH IMPERIALIST"

THE DAVE WHICH WAS NOT LOST
OR ALF

ON 7 MAY A KIYOKAWA MARU JAKE ON LONG-RANGE PATROL DISAPPEARED IN BAD WEATHER ALONG WITH A 6TH SENTAI CRUISER JAKE. ALLIED BOMBERS WERE SCOURING THE SAME AREAS SEARCHING FOR THE JAPANESE FLEET. THE NEXT DAY OF 8 MAY LT ARNOLD JOHNSON WAS CONDUCTING A SOLO PATROL IN A 40TH BS B-17E.

DANG THERE AIN'T DARN TOOTIN' OUT HERE

MAY AS WELL HEAD HOME EH FELLAS?

SEE ANYTHING AHEAD TOP TURRET?

JUDAS PRIEST! LOOK STRAIGHT AHEAD LIEUTENANT!

HOLY MUTHA OF GOD D'Y'ALL SEES WHAT I SEE?

THIS B-17E HAS A COLOURFUL 'HAWAIIAN AIR DEPOT' SCHEME

EEEASY BOYS, LET'S MOVE IN REAAL CLOSE

UNIDENTIFIED BIPLANE WAAAY IN DISTANCE

GUNNERS, CHARGE YOUR GUNS!

YESSIR!

SGT GEORGE RYAN IN WAIST GUN POSITION

JOHNSON, WHOSE NICKNAME WAS 'SKID', DESCENDED HIS B-17E TO 4,000 FEET WITHIN 400 YDS OF THE BIPLANE, IDENTIFIED AS A "TYPE 95" BIPLANE. THEN WAIST GUNNER RYAN FIRED 250 ROUNDS AT IT BEFORE IT RAPIDLY DIVED AWAY. THE EXCITED AMERICANS WERE CREDITED WITH THE KILL, HOWEVER NO JAPANESE FLOATPLANES WERE LOST THAT DAY. IT APPEARS THAT THE DAVE PILOT, WHOEVER HE WAS, SIMPLY DIVED AWAY EXPEDITIOUSLY FROM TROUBLE.

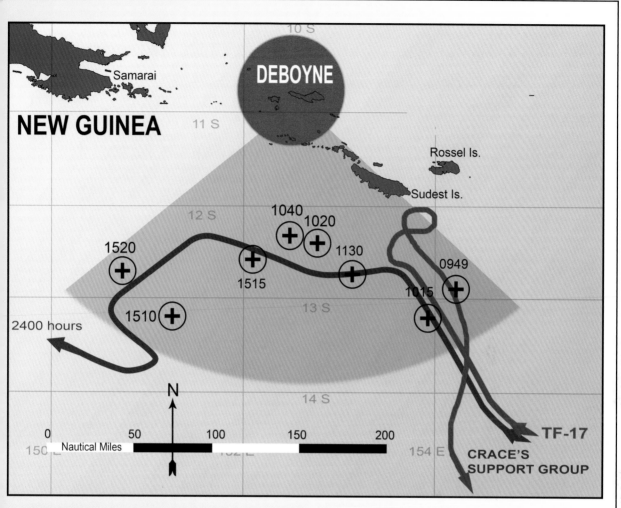

THE DEGREE TO WHICH THE 6TH SENTAI AND KIYOKAWA MARU FLOATPLANES WERE WIDELY SCATTERED AROUND THE OCEAN SOUTH OF DEBOYNE ON 7/8 MAY IS SHOWN ON THIS MAP. THESE ARE THEIR SIGHTINGS (AND TIMINGS) THEY MADE OF USN SHIP MOVEMENTS MADE ON 7 MAY ALONE.

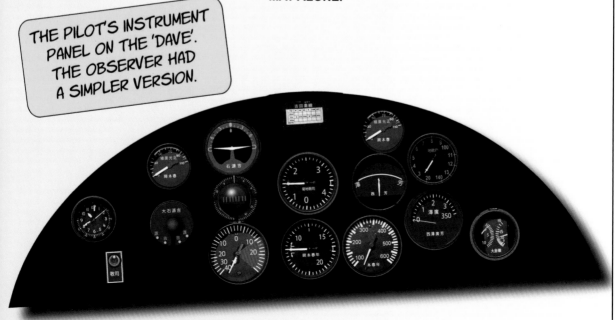

THE PILOT'S INSTRUMENT PANEL ON THE 'DAVE'. THE OBSERVER HAD A SIMPLER VERSION.

ON 9 MAY THE FLOATPLANE CONTINGENT AT DEBOYNE HAD UNWELCOME & POWERFUL VISITORS IN THE FROM OF THREE B-26 MARAUDER BOMBERS WHICH ATTACKED AT LOW LEVEL.

THESE, VERILY, WERE FAST & SLEEK ADVERSARIES.

GROWL . . .

ROAR! . . .

BLAM!

"TECHNICAL TERMS GALORE"

Propeller Speed
蝶旋機迴轉速度
rasenki kaiten sokudo

SECRET

Enemy Infiltration Techniques

ON MORNING OF 10 MAY THE MOST BIZARRE INCIDENT HAPPENED AT DEBOYNE, HOWEVER WE NEED TO GO BACK TO THE DAY BEFORE TO UNDERSTAND WHAT HAPPENED, AND WHY.

OH NOOO ! THIS DUDE IS FILLING A B-26 WITH DIESEL AND NOT 100 OCTANE!

7-MILE DROME PORT MORESBY

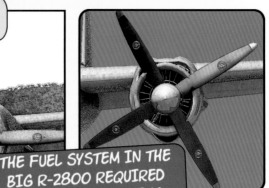

THE FUEL SYSTEM IN THE BIG R-2800 REQUIRED DRAINING + CLEANING

THE MASSIVE R-2800 HAD **18** CYLINDERS

ON 9 MAY A B-26 FLOWN BY LT RICHARD ROYALL WAS ACCIDENTALLY FILLED WITH DIESEL INSTEAD OF 100 OCTANE AT 7-MILE DROME, PREVENTING IT FROM PARTICIPATING IN A STRIKE AGAINST DEBOYNE THAT AFTERNOON. THE CREW WAS INSTRUCTED TO OVERNIGHT BEFORE RETURNING TO TOWNS-VILLE NEXT MORNING. ROYALL'S CREW WOULD ATTACK DEBOYNE ON THE WAY HOME. THEY TOOK OFF 10 MAY AT 0800 HOURS BUT WERE NEVER SEEN AGAIN. A FAULT WITH THE BOMBER'S BOMB RACKS MEANT THEY CARRIED NO BOMBS.

OK GUYS SO WE SNEAK IN A RIGHT HAND TURN HERE. WE'LL HIT DEBOYNE IN ABOUT TWO + A HALF HOURS

HOO BOY THIS PEA-SOUP IS WORSE THAN A NEW YORK FOG

ROYALL WAS PUSHING HIS BOMBER'S RANGE, SO LIKELY REDUCED POWER SETTINGS TO REDUCE FUEL CONSUMPTION

OTHER AIRCRAFT REPORTED BAD WEATHER AROUND THE TIP OF NEW GUINEA

DUDE, TIME TO POUR ON THE COAL. I CAN SEE DEBOYNE DEAD AHEAD

NEMOTO RECORDED THAT ROYALL'S B-26 ATTACKED AT 1230 MEANING IT TOOK THE B-26 THREE + HALF HOURS TO GET THERE

ROYALL'S CREW WAS INTENT ON SINGLE-HANDEDLY STRAFING DEBOYNE.
HOWEVER SPOTTERS THERE SAW THE B-26 APPROACHING WITH BINOCULARS . . . THE ACTIONS
OF THIS INTREPID & BRAVE CREW ARE UNDERLINED BY THE FACT THE B-26 WAS NOT EQUIPPED
FOR STRAFING MISSIONS, NOR DID IT CARRY BOMBS ON THIS MISSION . . .

ROYALL'S B-26 DROVE INTO THE LAGOON IN A SPLIT SECOND, KILLING ALL SEVEN ABOARD INSTANTLY, JUST OFFSHORE PANPOMPOM ISLAND.

THE BOMBER'S FATE WAS NOT DETERMINED UNTIL FOUR DECADES LATER, THROUGH JAPANESE RECORDS AND NEMOTO'S DIARY. THE NEW BOMBER WAS ONLY ON ITS SECOND MISSION.

FOLLOWING CLOSE BEHIND – A B-25 STRIKE!

DON'T SPARE THE AMMO Y'ALL HEAR!

PETE R-14 WAS THE MOST DAMAGED IN THE ATTACK

BLAM!

HOW GOOD IS THE MITSUBISHI SPECIALIST TOOLBOX?

WHILE THE SHOOT-DOWN BRIEFLY BOOSTED MORALE AT DEBOYNE, ONLY AN HOUR LATER SIX MITCHELLS DROPPED BOMBS FROM 5,500 FEET, WHICH FELL CLOSE TO THE FLOATPLANES ON THE BEACH, DAMAGING PETE R-14.

THE AMERICANS CONDUCTED MORE STRAFING BEFORE DUELLING WITH SEVERAL PETES & JAKES ALREADY AIRBORNE. THE MITCHELLS SUSTAINED 441 HITS FROM THE PASSES ALONG THE BEACH FLIGHTLINE. R-14 WAS FIXED THE FOLLOWING DAY ABOARD KIYOKAWA MARU.

BLAM!

NEMOTO IS HIDING BEHIND THIS PALM TREE

THE ATTACK FRIGHTENED NEMOTO,

"THE ENEMY RAID WAS SO TERRIFIC THAT I FELT MORE DEAD THAN ALIVE. I SOUVENIRED A FRAGMENT OF A 250 KG BOMB. EVERY TIME THERE WAS AN ATTACK WE RAN UNDER A TREE OR BEHIND A CONCRETE STRUCTURE. IT WAS SIMPLY BEYOND WORDS."

A MITCHELL NAMED *EL DIABLO* FOUGHT TWO FLOATPLANES DURING WHICH ITS LIFERAFT BROKE LOOSE, FLAPPING BADLY IN THE SLIPSTREAM. THE WAIST GUNNERS WERE UNABLE TO RETRIEVE IT, SO PILOT LT HAROLD MAULL FORCE-LANDED ON NEW GUINEA'S EASTERN TIP. THE CREW BURNED THE BOMBER, BUT NOT BEFORE MAULL SOUVENIRED THE CLOCK WHICH HE KEPT AS A MEMENTO.

EL DIABLO'S CREW WERE SOON RESCUED BY LUGGER.

ONE FLAPPING LIFE RAFT

EASY HAROLD MY-BOY, PUT THIS DEVIL DOWN REAAAAL EASY'N SWEET

GOSH, I CAN'T PULL IN THIS DANG FLAPPING DANGEROUS LIFE RAFT!

MAULL'S SOUVENIR EIGHT-DAY CLOCK (DURATION OF WINDING MECHANISM)

EL DIABLO

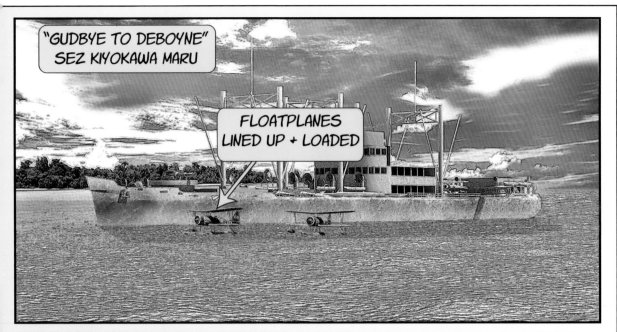

THE FLOATPLANE CONTINGENT AT DEBOYNE HAD BEEN TOLD THAT MORNING THAT PLANS HAD CHANGED AGAIN. ALL AIRCREW WERE TO PACK UP TO RETURN TO RABAUL. KIYOKAWA MARU SAILED EARLY NEXT MORNING OF 11 MAY, DETOURING THERE VIA SHORTLAND SEAPLANE BASE.

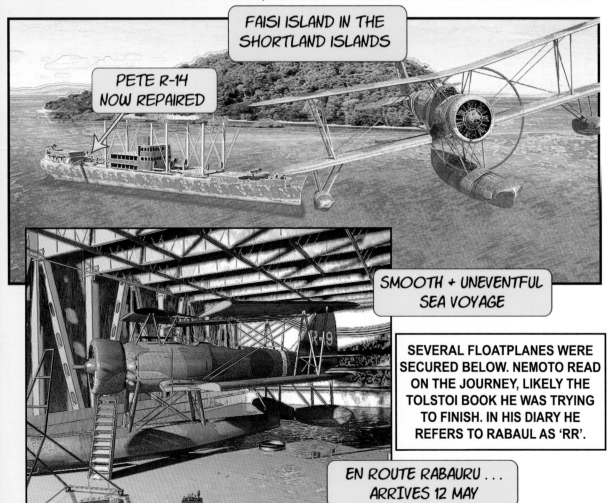

IJN ROUTINE AT MALAGUNA STARTS WITH REVILLE AT 0430 THEN ASSEMBLY TEN MINUTES LATER. BY 17 MAY SEVERAL PILOTS HAD CONTRACTED MALARIA, AND NEW ORDERS WERE ISSUED THAT FLIGHT SUITS WERE TO BE WORN WHILE SLEEPING TO REDUCE MOSQUITO BITE RISK. WORK ROUTINES CHANGED TOO, AS MORE GROUND DUTIES NEED TO BE PERFORMED. OUR HERO COMPLAINS HE IS NOT FLYING AS MUCH AS AIRCRAFT SERVICEABILITY IS DOWN.

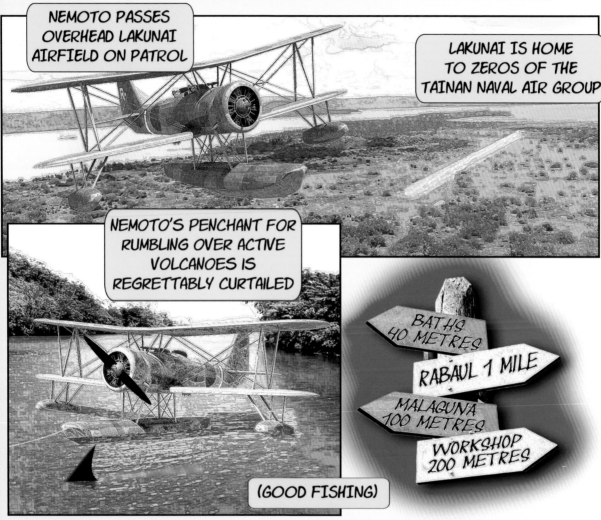

NEMOTO PASSES OVERHEAD LAKUNAI AIRFIELD ON PATROL

LAKUNAI IS HOME TO ZEROS OF THE TAINAN NAVAL AIR GROUP

NEMOTO'S PENCHANT FOR RUMBLING OVER ACTIVE VOLCANOES IS REGRETTABLY CURTAILED

BATHS 40 METRES

RABAUL 1 MILE

MALAGUNA 100 METRES

WORKSHOP 200 METRES

(GOOD FISHING)

ON 21 MAY NEMOTO DECRIES HIS NOW-MONOTONOUS LIFE, *"THERE ARE A COUPLE OF TRANS-FERS AMONG THE CREWS OWING TO ILLNESS. NOTHING TO REPORT ON PATROLS FROM MALAGUNA. NO ENEMY AIRCRAFT. WE ARE LEADING A DULL LIFE. I STILL ENJOY MY DAILY BATH"*.

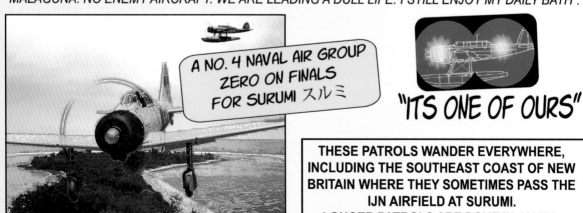

A NO. 4 NAVAL AIR GROUP ZERO ON FINALS FOR SURUMI スルミ

"ITS ONE OF OURS"

THESE PATROLS WANDER EVERYWHERE, INCLUDING THE SOUTHEAST COAST OF NEW BRITAIN WHERE THEY SOMETIMES PASS THE IJN AIRFIELD AT SURUMI. LONGER PATROLS ARE DONE IN JAKES.

THE WESTERN COASTLINE OF NEW BRITAIN

ONGOING PATROLS -BUSINESS AS USUAL- [YAWN]

ON 23 MAY NEMOTO IS ASSIGNED TO THE JAKE DETACHMENT FULL-TIME & CONDUCTS A THREE-HOUR PATROL FROM MALAGUNA. THREE DAYS LATER KIYOKAWA MARU SAILS FOR JAPAN. NEMOTO WRITES IT IS HARD THESEDAYS TO TAKE AFTERNOON SIESTA DUE TO THE HEAT.

ANOTHER DAY OF KEEPING RUFFIANS AT BAY . . .

ON 4 JUNE NEMOTO WRITES THAT HE IS TRYING TO REST AS MUCH AS POSSIBLE, AS A SECOND ATTEMPT TO TAKE PORT MORESBY COULD START SOON. HE UNDERSTANDS THAT KIYOKAWA MARU REACHED TRUK SAFELY THE EVENING BEFORE, AND IS DUE BACK IN RABAUL IN TWO DAYS TIME. HE PRAYS FOR THE SHIP'S SAFETY. NEMOTO COMPLAINS THAT EARLY THAT MORNING AROUND 0200 HOURS THEY HAD BEEN SUBJECTED TO A *"GUERILLA RAID"*

FOUR FORTRESSES CROSSING THE NEW BRITAIN COAST

"LOOK ALIVE LADS, LOOKS LIKE A BARRACKS AHEAD NEAR THAT RUNWAY"

IN FACT, USAAF RECORDS SHOW THAT THE BOMBS WERE DROPPED AT 0430 AND THAT VUNAKANAU AIRFIELD WAS ALSO A TARGET.

SEE THE BELOW CARTOGRAPHIC EXPOSÉ TO VISUALIZE THE LAYOUT OF THE AREA.

NEMOTO OBSERVES THAT THE IJN AT RABAUL IS EMBARRASSE DURING RAIDS, AND *"IN LAST NIGHT'S RAID THEY DROPPED FIVE OR SIX INCENDIARY BOMBS IN FRONT OF OUR UNIT'S BARRACKS. FORTUNATELY WE EXTINGUISHED THEM BEFORE A LARGE FIRE COULD BREAK OUT, BUT WE MUST NOT AGAIN BE CAUGHT OFF GUARD"*

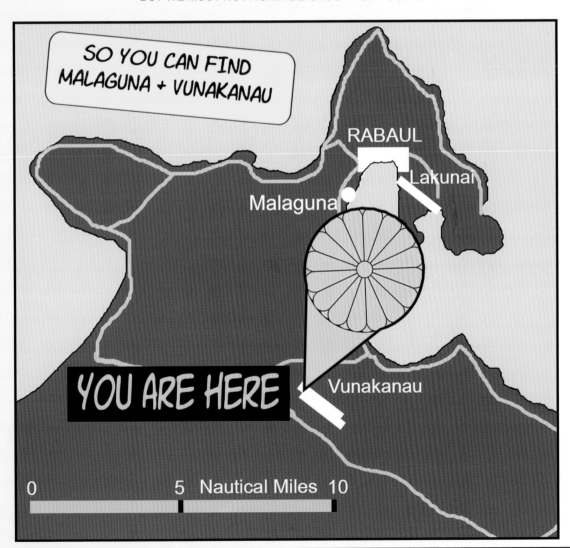

NOTE RED CODE Y-151 + WHITE BUNTAICHO STRIPE

THE 'ZERO FLOATPLANE' ASSIGNED TO BUNTAICHO LT SATO RI'ICHIRO

Editor's Comment: MC, Please remove this page is its entirety. It is nothing to do with Nemoto, and you are simply distracting the reader. The language is inopportune too.

EDITOR FIRED!

ON 5 JUNE NEMOTO DESCRIBES HOW AT 1000 HOURS THAT MORNING FIGHTER SEAPLANE "FIGHTERS" FLEW OVER RABAUL. THESE WERE A6M2-N RUFE FLOATPLANE FIGHTERS, RECENTLY RAISED BY THE YOKOHAMA NAVAL AIR GRAOUP AS A SEPARATE PURSUIT DETACHMENT, JUST ARRIVED AT RABAUL. THE UNIT SOON ADVANCED TO TULAGI TAKING SIXTEEN RUFES.

"SOOO ABOUT THE SWEET-AZ REALTY BELOW ME. . ."

NEW PILOT-DUDES EXPLORING RABAUL'S PURTY ENVIRONS

". . . MORE SUITED FOR HONEYMOONS THAN A DANG WAR."

AT ONE STAGE THESE NEW GUYS EVEN TRIED TO ATTACK A B-26, BUT COULD NOT CATCH IT.

RRRR-RRRRRR!

THESE BEASTS HAD THE MUTHAH OF ALL FLOATS

WE DIGRESS AT LEISURE BUT IN EDITORIAL PERIL, FOR IN REALITY NEMOTO HAD NOTHING TO DO WITH THESE NEWCOMER HERO FLYBOYS AS SOON HE WOULD BE OFF AGAIN . . .

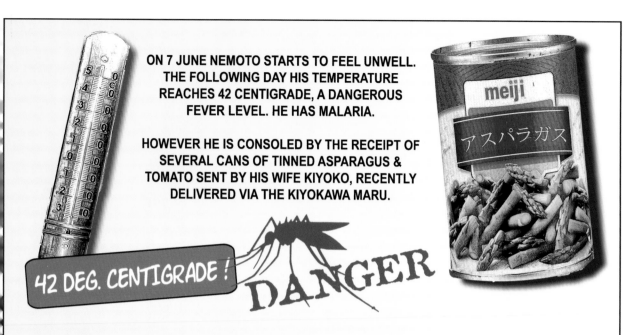

ON 7 JUNE NEMOTO STARTS TO FEEL UNWELL. THE FOLLOWING DAY HIS TEMPERATURE REACHES 42 CENTIGRADE, A DANGEROUS FEVER LEVEL. HE HAS MALARIA.

HOWEVER HE IS CONSOLED BY THE RECEIPT OF SEVERAL CANS OF TINNED ASPARAGUS & TOMATO SENT BY HIS WIFE KIYOKO, RECENTLY DELIVERED VIA THE KIYOKAWA MARU.

42 DEG. CENTIGRADE!

DANGER

MEANWHILE . . . . WAU WAS A MOUNTAIN TOWN BEHIND SALAMAUA WHOSE AIRFIELD HAD BEEN ESTABLISHED IN THE 1930S TO SUPPLY NEARBY GOLDFIELDS. IN LATE MAY, AFTER BATTLE OF CORAL SEA, MORE AUSTRALIAN TROOPS WERE FLOWN INTO WAU, EVEN THOUGH THE SMALL TOWN WAS ONLY ABOUT 50 MILES FROM JAPANESE-OCCUPIED LAE!

AN EARLY MORNING DEPARTURE FROM SEVEN-MILE DROME NEAR PORT MORESBY

THE MIGHTY OWEN STANLEY RANGES

A C-47 TRANSPORT OF THE USAAF 21ST TRANSPORT SQUADRON

HEY HANK, HOPE WE DOAN MEET NO ZEROS TODAY NEAR WAU

YEAH, SURE WISH WE HAD OUR AIRACOBRA FRIENDS WITH US 2DAY

THE APPROACH INTO WAU WAS DANGEROUS. IT WAS A 'ONE WAY' STRIP MEANING ONCE COMMITTED, THE TRANSPORTS HAD TO LAND. AT THE END OF THE INCLINED STRIP WAS A MOUNTAIN.

BANKING OVER THE BULOLO VALLEY

THE MOUNTAINS IN THE MORNING WERE USUALLY SHROUDED IN CLOUD

ABOARD THESE C-47S WERE MORE BAD-ASS AUSTRALIAN COMMANDOS

ON FINALS INTO WAU

THIS DUDE WAS PHOTOGRAPHED AT BUNA

BY JUNE THE AUSTRALIAN TROOPS AT WAU, KNOWN COLLECTIVELY AS KANGA FORCE, HAD GROWN SEVERAL HUNDRED STRONG & INCLUDED A COMPANY OF COMMANDOS. THEY PLANNED A RAID AGAINST THE JAPANESE GARRISON AT SALAMAUA, ACCURATELY ESTIMATED TO HOLD 250 JAPANESE.

MAKE NO MISTAKE - THESE AUSSIE COMMANDOS ARE SERIOUS DUDES

"YET ANOTHER USEFUL PHRASE"

Piston Ring

「ピストンリング」

pisuton ringu

NEMOTO IS SUFFICIENTLY ILL THAT HE MAKES NO DIARY ENTRIES FOR NEARLY TWO WEEKS. THE MALARIA HAS REALLY HIT HIM HARD. ON 21 JUNE HE REJUVENATES HIS DIARY BY WRITING THAT HE HAD RECEIVED A MAGAZINE FROM HIS FRIEND "NISHIMURA". HE ALSO RECEIVED A LETTER FROM HIS WIFE KIYOKO WHICH SHE POSTED IN JAPAN EXACTLY TEN DAYS PRIOR. HE IS CONCERNED WHEN SHE TELLS HIM SHE HAS TO QUEUE IN JAPAN TO PURCHASE FOOD. THE NEXT DAY AT MALAGUNA ALL FLOATPLANE PILOTS ARE TOLD THEY ARE TO SOON RECEIVE A "SPECIAL 100 PER CENT BONUS" IN RECOGNITION OF THEIR EFFORTS TO DATE.

MORE ¥

REMEMBER THIS PHOTO FROM THE BEGINNING? THIS IS NEMOTO'S BOSS, LT TAKEDA SHIGEKI.

SO, ON 25 JUNE AN AIRCREW DETACHMENT AT MALAGUNA WAS ORDERED TO SALAMAUA NEXT MORNING

TWO PETE FLOATPLANES FLEW TO SALAMAUA EARLY NEXT MORNING. NEMOTO, AS DETACHMENT LEADER, WOULD FOLLOW.

NEMOTO DEPARTED IN A 4TH FLEET MAVIS WHICH DEPARTED RABAUL ON 28 JUNE AT 0800 HOURS.

GREEEAT. SO HOW MANY COCONUTS CAN I COUNT?

THE FINSCHHAFEN SHORELINE HAD MANY COCONUT PLANTATIONS, + VILLAGES WITH PURTY NAMES LIKE BESUGA + KWALANSAM

THIS GREY SANDY SHORELINE HAD MANY VILLAGES WITH NAMES LIKE SALUS, LAUKANU, BOISI AND BUAKAP.

SOUTH OF SALAMAUA WAS BEAUTIFUL LASANGA ISLAND

KELA VILLAGE WHERE BAD DUDES ARE GATHERING

THIS IDYLLIC SETTING ON EVENING 28 JUNE IS BETRAYED BY THE ASSEMBLY OF THE AUSSIE RUFFIANS YONDER

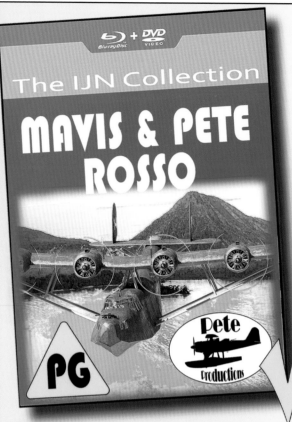

WITH ALL THIS ADVENTUROUS ACTIVITY IN THE OBSCURE & RUGGED LANDS OF PAPUA & NEW GUINEA, WHAT A PITY THERE IS NO SERIES ALONG THE LINES OF THE HYPOTHENTICAL PRODUCTION ILLUSTRATED OPPOSITE, WHERE THE SCENARY IS CERTAINLY EQUAL TO THAT OF THE ADRIATIC.

OF COURSE, DVD & BLU-RAY FORMATS ARE 'OLD HAT'. PERHAPS SOMEONE CAN TALK NETFLIX INTO A WONDROUS PRODUCTION?

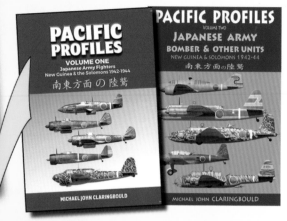

FORTUNATELY THERE IS SOME RESPITE. IF YOU HAVE ANY INTEREST IN THE ACCURATE HISTORY OF THE PACIFIC AIR WAR, WHERE BOTH SIDES' RECORDS ARE CONSULTED, THEN LOOK NO FURTHER THAN THE SERIES OF BOOKS PUBLSIHED BY AVONMORE BOOKS. THERE IS EVEN A 'PROFILES' SERIES WHICH PORTRAY ACCURATE MARKINGS. THE BOOK ON 'OPERATION I-GO' IS HIGHLY DETAILED, AND SO IS THE 'PACIFIC ADVERSARIES' SERIES.

YAMAMOTO'S APRIL 1943 OPERATION, CITING ADMIRAL KUSAKA'S DIARY + OTHER RARE PRIMARY DOCUMENTS

THE 'ADVERSARY' SERIES LINES UP COMBATANTS ONE-ON-ONE, GIVING CRACKING TALES + UNIQUE DETAIL

SHAMELESS ADVETISING, YES, DERIVED FROM PRIDE IN QUALITY

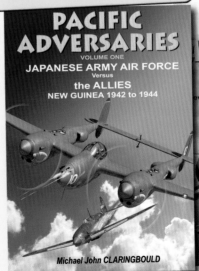

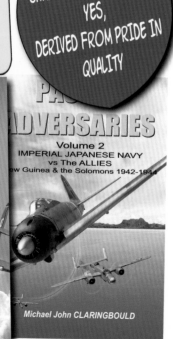

BACK TO 28 JUNE AND NEMOTO ABOARD A MAVIS EN ROUTE TO SALAMAUA

SKIRTING THE COAST OF NEW BRITAIN

HUMMMMMM
[ENGINE NOISE]

APART FROM CLIMBING OVER THE NEW BRITAIN MOUNTAIN SPINE, MOST OF THE FLIGHT OVER OCEAN WAS MADE AT LOWER ALTITUDES TO AVOID ENEMY DETECTION.

THESE SEAPLANE PILOTS OF THE 4TH FLEET TRANSPORT SECTION KNEW THEIR BUSINESS. THEY FLEW H6K4 MAVIS FROM JAPAN TO DESTINATIONS ALL OVER THE PACIFIC. THE DUDES UP FRONT HAD BEEN TO SALAMAUA SEVERAL TIMES. FOR THEM, THIS WAS THE JAPANESE DEFINITION OF A 'MILK RUN'

APPROACHING SALAMAUA . . .

HUMMMMMM
[ENGINE NOISE]

THE BEAUTIFUL PEACEFUL ISTHMUS OF SALAMAUA . . .

NEMOTO RECORDED THAT THEY DEPLANED AT 'RZL' – CODENAME OF SALAMAUA – AT EXACTLY 1220

IP IN THE HILLS. . .

AUSTRALIAN SPIES !

HOWEVER AS THEY DISEMBARKED, THEY WERE NOT TO KNOW THAT THEY WERE BEING CAREFULLY WATCHED BY AUSSIE COASTWATCHES, SECURED IN A SECRET OBSERVATION POST IN THE HILLS BEHIND SALAMAUA.

THRU THE BINOCULARS THEY COULD EVEN READ THE TAILCODE L-06

THE AUSTRALIAN SPIES NOTED ELEVEN MEN DISEMBARK, ALONG WITH COLOURED STRAW SUITCASES, ROUND BAGS AND A BOX, *"ABOUT 15 INCHES SQUARE. THIS BOX WAS COVERED WITH A WHITE CLOTH AND THE OBJECTS IN THE BOX HELD THE CLOTH ABOUT 4 TO 6 INCHES ABOVE THE BOX LEVEL. AN OFFICER NURSED THIS BOX FROM THE FLYING BOAT TO THE WHARF, THIS BOX WAS THEN CARRIED TO THE COMMANDER'S HOUSE . . ."*

NEMOTO + FRIENDS HAD BEEN SENT TO SUPPORT AN IMPERIAL ARMY UNIT HEADED BY A LT OKABE

HUT ON SALAMAUA FORESHORE

WONDER WOT WOZ IN BOX?

THE SIGN READS "OKABE DETACHMENT HQ" PART OF THE SASEBO NO 5 SPECIAL NAVAL LANDING FORCES

EVENING OF 28 JUNE

BAD-ASS AUSSIE COMMANDOS AT KELA VILLAGE, NEAR SALAMAUA

THE RAID ON SALAMAUA COMMENCED IN THE EARLY HOURS OF 29 JUNE. IT PROVED A TEXTBOOK COMMANDO OPERATION. IN THE DARKNESS & CONFUSION THE AUSSIES ESTIMATED THEY KILLED ABOUT ONE HUNDRED JAPANESE. WHILE THE ACTUAL COUNT WAS EIGHTEEN, THE CAPTURED EQUIPMENT & DOCUMENTS PROVED INVALUABLE FOR INTELLIGENCE PURPOSES.

THE ATTACK COMMENCED AT 0200 HOURS. AN EXPLOSION FROM THE DIRECTION OF KELA VILLAGE PRESAGED THE AUSTRALIAN CHARGE THROUGH SALAMAUA. SHOCKED JAPANESE SCUTTLED FROM THE HOUSES IN SLEEPING ATTIRE, STUMBLING TOWARDS SHELTERS AND TRENCHES. GALLANT FLOATPLANE HERO, NEMOTO, WAS ONE OF THE EIGHTEEN KILLED.